THE ACOL SYSTEM

THE
ACOL SYSTEM
of
CONTRACT
BRIDGE

by

BEN COHEN and TERENCE REESE

FOURTH EDITION

With S. J. Simon's introduction to the Third Edition
Completely revised, with three new chapters
and
an Appendix illustrating

THE SYSTEM AT WORK

in the International Series of 1949

Price 10s 6d

PUBLISHED BY
JOINER AND STEELE LTD
102A SOUTHAMPTON ROW . LONDON

First Published, January, 1938

Revised and Enlarged Edition, February, 1939

Third Edition (with 12 hands
from Waddington's Par Contests), June 1946

Fourth Edition (with a selection of
Hands from the 1949 International Series),
November, 1949

Printed in Great Britain by
KNIGHT AND FORSTER LTD
WATER LANE WORKS · LEEDS II

AUTHORS' FOREWORD TO
THE FOURTH EDITION

AS we explained in the Foreword to the previous editions, the presentation of the Acol system in this book does not set out to be a self-contained treatise on bidding. It assumes knowledge on the part of the reader of the Approach Forcing system and for the most part is concerned with explaining how Acol players interpret the Approach Forcing method, and what special variations they have introduced.

In addition to some new examples in the text, there are three completely new chapters in this edition. The two chapters on Competitive Bidding and on Some Mistakes to Avoid are of general interest and apply to bidding on any system. The chapter on the new Two Club response introduces an important convention which is still in the exploratory stage and should be regarded as optional for Acol players.

Attention must be drawn to the change in the interpretation of a pass after a redouble by third hand, described in Chapter XI.

Some critics reviewing the last edition made the comment that there was nothing in the book to show that the Acol system was anything other than the invention of the authors. Let it be repeated, then, that in the successive editions of this book we do a job of reporting. The small changes which we introduce from time to time represent the development of the system among the leading players who use it.

The Acol system stands to-day as high as ever. A system such as the Baron appears at first sight to be more accurate than Acol and to give players fuller guidance for determining their bids. Experience has shown, however, that the advantages, such as they are, of systems which define principles of bidding more precise than those of Acol, tend to disappear in practical play because those systems are more difficult to play accurately.

It is a nice point, to what extent the virtues of a bidding system can be separated from the idiosyncrasies of those who practice them. The small group of players who use the Baron system are amongst the best in the country, but when they run up against the best Acol players in straight matches, they do not seem to gain points in the bidding : this, despite the fact that Acol players readily agree that many bidding sequences in Baron have an exactness to which Acol makes no claim. But the Baron players seem to make so many more mistakes. They find it difficult to play their own system well. Acol players don't. There must be a moral somewhere.

THE SYSTEM AT WORK

A special feature of this edition is the inclusion of a selection of hands, illustrating the system at work in the match between Crockfords and America for the Crowninshield Cup and in the European Championships of 1949, won, for the second year in succession by the British team, playing the Acol system.

B.C.
J.T.R.

October, 1949

INTRODUCTION

ATTITUDE OF MIND
by S. J. SIMON

THE Acol system has often been described as an attitude of mind. It is high time this attitude was set down in print, for, judging by their constantly suggested improvements which have to be firmly sat on, a great many alleged Acol exponents don't even begin to possess it. It is never easy to explain an attitude, but I feel that I must have a stab at explaining this one.

The Acol attitude comes half-way between two schools of thought. The first and most popular school, whom I call the scientists, believe that bidding is essentially a duet between partners, an exact science subject to immutable laws, and that the more one learns of those laws the more accurate will bidding become. The second school, still flourishing in the North, believes in no conventions and common sense, the more you have got the more you bid, and, when hard-pressed in argument, that all these feature-showing conventions are nothing but cheating anyway and, in the words of Mr. James Agate, there is no difference between them and looking at your wrist watch to tell partner you hold all four Aces. What Mr. Agate of course ignores is that bidding, say, a conventional four no-trumps uses up a tempo, while looking at your wrist watch does not.

The Acol attitude has realised that bidding is not an exact science but a scientific estimation of mathematical probabilities. It has also realised that the probabilities to be estimated include the probable actions of opponents, who regrettably happen to be present, and that the entire language for estimating is limited to thirty-five bids (one club to seven no-trumps), and that that is not nearly enough to paint a complete picture of the hand most of the time or even part of the time. It has therefore realised that there is a limit to the accuracy any system can reach and that no system can hope to be completely accurate all the time.

Accordingly, it has thrown that particular ambition into the gutter, where the scientists can scramble for it, and set itself out to evolve a loose flexible style of bidding, which, though not as accurate as some systems on certain types of hands, will in the long run achieve better results over all types of hands both by the aid of its own bidding machinery and opponent's mistakes.

Opponent's mistakes !

These words form an essential element of the Acol attitude. But the scientists do not appear even to envisage that they can happen.

Recently I found a bunch of them clustered round a hand published by Ewart Kempson in the *Star*.

♠ 10.x.x.x.x.x
♡ K.x.x
◇ x.x.x
♣ x

♠ A.K.J.x.x
♡ A.J.10.9
◇ A.Q
♣ A.10

The late Colonel Walter Buller had played this hand in six spades against an opening lead of the king of clubs. Winning the trick with ace, he drew trumps, played the ten of clubs and when West covered with the jack, let him hold it discarding a heart from the dummy.

Kempson had been rightly enthusiastic about Buller's line of play but the scientists were sceptical and were busily discussing percentage angles, distributional frequencies and what-nots in an effort to prove a simple heart finesse through East offered the better chance. Whether or not they were right mathematically, I would not know.   Buller fails while they succeed against hearts Q.x.x.x or hearts Q.x.x.x.x in East's hand, while Buller succeeds and they fail against Q.x.x with West. Both fail against hearts Q.x.x.x with West.   Mathematically it is clearly extremely close.

But in practice there is no argument but that Buller's line of play was correct.   Because while the scientist's line of play gives opponents no chance to go wrong, Buller offered both East and West a first-class opportunity to chuck by playing a heart.

First West on play does not know whether to lead hearts or diamonds, and if he leads diamonds — that's that ! And if he leads hearts and East holds queen to four, then East must play low or he will present declarer with the contract.

And how many Easts do you know who could be guaranteed to play low in this situation ?

But this aspect of the Colonel's play had inevitably never even occurred to the scientists.   It never does occur to them to think about opponents !

Opponents will make mistakes.   Further, opponents can be encouraged to make mistakes.   If they don't make mistakes you won't win many matches.   But the Acol is the only system I know that consciously devotes a part of its machinery to encouraging opponents into errors. There are other systems that are difficult to play against — natural bidders for instance are a nightmare to oppose. But it is an accidental nightmare arising out of the general slovenliness of their methods and not a planned nightmare.

You don't know what to do against them because these bidders so often don't know what they're doing.

Acol bidders always know exactly what they're doing. Their machinery often puts opponents on a spot from which they have to guess while the partnership knows its own combined strength to within a point.

This is known as making life difficult for the enemy and easy for yourself.

As I have so often pointed out and will no doubt be pointing out again, there are two objectives in Bridge. The first is to make the best of your cards, the second to prevent the enemy making the best of theirs. The first is clearly the more important, that is why a certain amount of scientifically planned bidding machinery is necessary to a system. But to ignore the second entirely, as the scientists do, is to ignore the major element of Bridge. The competitive element.

If you think about the matter at all you must realise at once that when one is talking of a par result on a hand one is talking not of the maximum points that can be scored by the winning side but of the minimum points that must be lost by the losing side. And that the only cases where these two come to the same thing are the deals where the combined strength of your hands is such that the enemy are powerless to interfere with the result. A deal which is independent of the way opponents bid or play their cards. Or, in other words, the sort of deal where it does not matter if your opponents are Culbertson and Lightner or Mr. and Mrs. Jones from across the road.

And the bulk of bridge hands are not like that, fortunately.

Most of the time what the enemy is doing, or may do, must be given some attention.

The point is, how much attention?

For any attention that is given can only be given at

the risk of your own accuracy. That is obvious enough. When you make an ordinary pre-emptive bid to hamper opponents, you are immediately lessening the chances of finding your own best contract. If you knew in advance that partner held a " two club " bid, you wouldn't do it. But as the chances are that he doesn't, you make it because it is more probable that your bid will annoy opponents than embarrass partner.

The Acol attitude believes that this theory of probabilities should be borne in mind throughout the whole gamut of bidding, and that even at low levels there are situations where it will pay on balance to withhold information from partner and risk missing the best contract, rather than tell partner something which may be of no value to him and risk opponents profiting from it.

This has nothing to do with system or system bids. It is entirely an attitude of mind which believes that in the long run a perpetual bit of extra puzzle to the enemy is more profitable than a bulk of mainly useless information to partner.

The scientists don't share this attitude. They believe exactly the opposite. They think the number of times the extra information will get them into the right contract will more than compensate for the extra opportunities given to the opponents.

If you agree with them, don't play Acol. You're wasting your time and your horrible results don't help the system.

Consider the following hand.

♠ None
♡ A.10.x.x
♢ K.x.x
♣ A.K.Q.10.x.x

Both scientists and Acolites will open the bidding of

this hand with one club, the scientists because it is the scientific approach and the Acolites because at this stage there are too many possibilities about this hand to rush blindly into five clubs or three no-trumps. At this stage the risk of opponents getting together just has to be taken. Natural bidders, who probably open this hand with three clubs, minimise that risk, but replace it with the dilemna of what to do if, as he most probably will, partner bids three no-trumps, and are unlikely to show a profit on their guesses.

Now, supposing over one club, next hand passes, partner bids two clubs, and next hand bids two diamonds. What do you bid now?

If you bid two hearts — don't play Acol.

There is nothing wrong with the bid as a book bid. In fact it is without doubt the correct book bid. Four hearts or three no-trumps may well be the best contract on the hand. There may even be a slam in clubs in it if partner holds exactly the right cards, for instance :—

♠ x.x.x.x
♡ K.Q.x
◇ x.x
♣ J.x.x.x

Bidding two hearts gives you the opportunity to investigate all these possibilities. So what's wrong with it?

The answer, you ass, is the opponents. It is at least a hundred to one on that over two hearts next hand will bid two spades, paving the way to a probable cheap save or, worse still, a successful contract of their own. Your partner's spades at the best are K.x.x.x, else he would have bid them, and now that he has supported clubs, your hand isn't so hot in defence. You cannot even guarantee defeating six spades. Your king of diamonds may not be a trick; players have bid suits without holding the ace.

But if over the two diamond butt-in you bid five clubs

you will almost certainly put a stop to all that nonsense. It may not be absolutely the best contract on the hand but your chances of making it, even if it isn't on, must be very high. If the hand over you holds the ace of diamonds it is unlikely not to lead it.

Anybody who believes that a bid of two hearts on this type of hand and bidding will in the long run show a profit over five clubs had better take this book to the store where he bought it and try to swop it for some system that will order him about and permit him to leave his judgement at home.

But, if you would have bid five clubs, or three no-trumps or any other enemy hampering fantasy, then you can study the following pages with profit. For there you will find the system that has been built to fit the attitude. A system with a few set pivotal bids, a minimum of forced responses, and the maximum of room for manoeuvring as the logic of the situation dictates. A system concentrated on the bidding of everyday hands in a manner to combine a sufficient accuracy with the best chance of harassing opponents. A system rich in light opening bids and even richer in sign offs, always ready to start one jump ahead of opponents, and equipped with masses of brakes for back pedalling if the jump gets too dangerous. A system resigned to occasional bad results, because it is aiming at the best results on balance and will not squander any of its machinery on the occasional big hands when it can more profitably be applied to the bidding of the much more frequent every-day hands.

In short a system for Bridge players and not for parrots.

One final word of advice. There is no need to treat everything in the text as gospel. Acol is not that rigid. There will always, from time to time, be minor amendments to the rules. If you don't like them, ignore them. Depart from the system whenever the situation seems to you to demand it.

But never depart from the attitude.

CONTENTS

CHAPTER I

A GENERAL VIEW OF THE SYSTEM

ACOL is a composite system but a complete unity within itself. Its main structure is that of the Culbertson approach-forcing system, and although it includes a conventional two club bid, it should be classified with the one-over-one rather than with the two club systems. The main feature of the latter is that they employ an opening bid of two in a suit for hands of intermediate strength so that an opening bid of one is necessarily limited in strength ; but Acol uses two bids, other than two clubs, for hands of a particular character, corresponding to the Culbertson two-way three bid rather than to the two bid of orthodox two club systems ; while opening bids of one may be of great strength, as in the forcing two. This allows the opening bid of three to be reserved for weak hands containing a long suit ; the bid is purely pre-emptive.

MAIN ELEMENTS

There are thus four main elements in Acol. These are :—

1.—*The Approach method* of the Culbertson system forming the basic structure of the system.

2.—*The Acol Two Bid*, reserved for hands of great playing strength, which for one reason or another constitute a problem in the forcing two system, which has no opening other than a bid of one or a bid of two forcing to game. The Acol two is forcing for one round only.

3.—*The Acol Two Club Bid*, which is made on hands of game-going strength, containing not fewer than five honour tricks ; the bid is forcing to game.

4.—*The Weak Three Bid*, as used in the four aces system but excluded from the Culbertson system by the use of the two-way three bid. An opening of three on the Acol is so weak as to be simply a gambit ; it suggests from five to six playing tricks.

The advantage of Acol is that it contains the best of all the good systems. The originators of the system discovered, some years before Culbertson conceded the point with the introduction of the two-way three bid, that *a third opening bid is required* beside the bid of one and the bid of two forcing to game. Let the Culbertsonians say what they will, there are some hands which on the system are too strong for a bid of One, and yet are unsafe forcing bids ; these are the hands of unbalanced distribution which require a particular queen or jack in partner's hand to make game a near certainty ; and there are some hands which although they can be safely opened at the range of one constitute an insoluble problem at the second round of bidding. For example, you hold :—

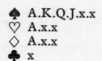

Playing the strong two but not the two-way three bid (which would make matters still more difficult), you open, as you must, One Spade. That is all right, as it is unlikely that you can get game if partner cannot respond to one spade, but suppose that your partner responds two hearts or two diamonds ; now what do you do ? The trouble is that you have underbid on the first round in saying one spade, and you are now completely at a loss for a bid which will indicate the character of your hand and give you a chance of finding the best contract. You dare not bid less than game ; three spades is a very strong bid on the Culbertson system, but it can be passed, and if you take a chance on this the probable response of three no-trumps won't help you ; four spades may lead to a missed slam as for all your partner knows your hand might be of an entirely different character, something like :—

♠ K.Q.J.10.x.x.x
♡ K.x
◇ A.10.x
♣ x

All you want in partner's hand is five diamonds to the K.Q to make the slam an odds-on chance, and you have no time to find out what he has. The best you can do is to bid an immediate four no-trumps, and over five diamonds say five spades ; then if partner's diamonds are weak, you will go one down on a heart lead, and be able to blame nothing but the system. The Acol two bid would have got you right out of your difficulties ; you would open two spades, making it clear at once that you have eight playing tricks ; partner would say three diamonds, you three spades, and partner probably three no-trumps ; you make a slam try with four diamonds, and partner would appreciate that you held the ace, and a fine hand. If partner still signed off with four spades, you would give in, confident that you had missed no slam.

The two club bid itself is an excellent weapon for hands of great honour strength. A minimum of five quick tricks is guaranteed, so that the hand is at once distinguished from the hands of great distributional strength which on Culbertson sometimes have to be opened with a bid of two. The weakness response of two diamonds by the responding hand has the advantage of permitting a non-forcing two no-trump rebid, and furthermore, it avoids exposing the strong hand when the contract is played in no-trumps.

Finally the use of the conventional two club bid permits the opening bidder, who has a strong, balanced hand, to show his exact strength with an accuracy which is not possible on any other system. Four methods of bidding are possible, an opening of two no-trumps, of three no-trumps, of two clubs followed by two no-trumps, and of two clubs followed by three no-trumps. Every one of these bidding procedures has a precise meaning in the Acol system.

PLAYING STRENGTH AND OPENING BIDS

The existence of perfect machinery to deal with strong hands has a natural effect upon opening bids. It is a disadvantage of the Culbertson system that in the absence of more than one bid to deal with strong hands, light openings, except when partner has passed, are impractical. Because the opening bid may be on a hand of exceptional strength the whole structure of bidding is based on gradual development in which every change of suit is almost forcing and a single rebid is a sign of strength, rather than a denial of greater strength. This is the essence of the approach method and so far as it goes it is excellent. Its disadvantage is that it rules out those opening bids which are based on playing strength rather than honour strength, and which are a feature of natural bidding and of the Lederer two club system. The $2\frac{1}{2}$ honour trick regulation is very necessary on the Culbertson system, *which is much less rich in sign-off bids than Acol;* but for Acol players it has no meaning whatsoever as a standard for opening bids. The tactical advantage of opening the bidding is not in dispute among experienced players, and at Acol light openings can be made danger to the general process of constructive bidding.

CHAPTER II

OPENING BIDS OF ONE

A S was explained in the first chapter the basic structure of the Acol system is that of the Culbertson approach forcing system. The Acol two bid and the two club itself are speciality bids, in no way interfering with the general character of the approach forcing method. Opening bids of one in the Acol system cover as wide a range of honour trick strength as in Culbertson; indeed they cover a wider range, for the 2½ honour trick stipulation has no place in Acol; almost any hand containing a six-card suit and about 10 points on the popular count of 4 for an ace, 3 for a king, 2 for a queen, and 1 for a jack, qualifies for a bid on Acol; the following hands should all be opened with a bid of one, irrespective of vulnerability:

♠ K.8.7.6.4.2	♠ K.10.6
♡ A.7.5	♡ 3
♢ Q.3.2	♢ Q.6.5
♣ 4	♣ A.J.9.7.6.4

♠ 10.5	♠ K.Q.10.6.4
♡ K.9.5	♡ A.J.7.6.3
♢ J.4	♢ 7.4
♣ K.Q.J.10.6.5	♣ 8

The purpose of opening on these hands should not be misunderstood. The two which contain good major suits might lead to a game which would be missed if the hand were passed, but this cannot be said of the two club hands. The main reason for opening is that at all times an opening

bid is the best defence, so that provided the opening is
sound, containing a safe re-bid, the bid should be made
without hesitation.

THE SAFETY FACTOR IN LIGHT OPENINGS

It is most important that the meaning of the last section
should not be over-simplified to the point of assuming that
it is a regular feature of Acol to open the bidding on hands
which are about half a trick under strength on any other
system. The following hands are *not* proper opening bids :—

♠ K.x.x.x.x	♠ A.K.x.x
♡ A.Q.x	♡ x.x
◇ x.x	◇ Q.x.x.x.x
♣ Q.x.x	♣ Q.x

♠ x.x	♠ A.Q.x.x.x
♡ Q.x.x.x.x	♡ x.x.x
◇ A.K.x.x.x	◇ A.x
♣ x	♣ x.x.x

A comparison between this group of hands and the group
above, on which an opening was recommended, will show
what great importance is attached to the sixth card of the
trump suit.

The argument on the *former* group of hands is this :—
" While it is true that the hand is weak in honour
tricks, it is nevertheless impossible that the opening
bid can come to any serious harm. The system of
sign-off bids in Acol is so well planned that there is
every chance of arresting the bidding process before
the range of possible contracts has been passed. If the
eventual contract is defeated by a few tricks, it is at
least certain that the enemy have been robbed of a
game or part score. Furthermore, if the hand is passed
now and partner opens the bidding, it may be difficult

to communicate to him the extent of playing strength concealed by the previous pass."

But on the second group of hands the argument should be :—

" To open now is to undermine the whole fabric of constructive bidding. No safety valve exists in the shape of a long trump suit which will make possible a sign-off. Whatever final contract is reached is as likely to be defeated as on the other group of hands, and it may no longer be the case that the defeated contract will represent a worth-while sacrifice. In a word, it now becomes more dangerous to open, while the advantages of opening and securing the contract are less than before."

That an aggressive policy for opening bids is of great advantage especially in the part score range is generally acknowledged ; but it does not pay to open the bidding when the most likely result is a two or three trick penalty and nothing saved.

USE OF PREPARED BIDS

In common with all the approach forcing systems Acol follows the one-over-one principle in respect of responses in a new suit, which are forcing for one round. A sound rebid is therefore essential in face of any suit response, so that to a certain extent prepared bids must be included in the system. Whenever possible, an Acol player prefers to bid his cards in the natural order, and he is always anxious to avoid the manœuvre, so dear to a host of approach bidders, of opening the suit which will pave the way most readily for partner's expected response.

Do not, therefore, look at your hand and say : " Now what is partner most likely to bid ? One heart ? Then I will open one diamond, although I have five spades and four diamonds."

Put the question to yourself in this way : " Does the necessity of having a sound rebid in face of any suit response compel me to bid my cards other than in the most natural way ?"

♠ K.J.x.x
♥ x.x.x
♦ A.Q.x
♣ A.10.x

Not vulnerable, this hand can be opened one no-trump. Vulnerable, one club must be endured, for one spade affords no sound re-bid over two hearts.

A very important safeguard is attached to the prepared opening of one club. The shorter suit having been opened, the rebid on the hand must be in no-trumps, not in another suit. This is to prevent the ignominy of being given preference in a suit which one does not prefer.

♠ Q.x.x.x
♥ K.J.x.x
♦ A.x
♣ K.J.x

There is no escape, if vulnerable, from a one club opening, for a 14 point hand is too good to pass and to open one heart and rebid two no-trumps over two diamonds is too unsound. If over one club partner bids one diamond, the rebid must be one no-trump and not one heart, for if the latter is bid, partner may jump in clubs ; he is quite entitled to do so, for at Acol it should always be assumed that partner is bidding his cards naturally, and if he is not, it is his responsibility.

♠ J.9.3
♥ A.K.8.7
♦ J.10.2
♣ A.J.6

This is a hand from a Par Contest and wonder was expressed by some competitors that an opening bid of one heart was recommended. Well, the choice is between one heart and no bid, for to say one club (vulnerability ruling out one no-trump) is revolting to an Acol player; after all, the rebid of two no-trump over two diamonds is only a slight overbid, and especially as the situation may well not arise, it is surely a better solution to open one heart and let the future look to itself.

♠ A.K.10.x
♡ J.x
♢ K.Q.x.x
♣ K.x.x

Most approach bidders would open one diamond " to anticipate a heart response "; what advantage is conferred by this anticipation is obscure, and an Acol player should bid one spade, as there is a perfectly good two no-trump rebid over two hearts.

♠ A.K.x.x
♡ K.10.x.x.x
♢ Q.x
♣ x.x

The prepared bid of one spade (made to avoid a reverse on such a moderate hand) is acceptable here.

♠ K.Q.x.x
♡ A.10.9.8.7
♢ x.x
♣ Q.x

Now it is better to open one heart and over two of a minor say two hearts. If partner cannot bid again, no game will be missed, and the disadvantage of opening one spade is

that over two hearts one may get a jump preference to three
or even four spades on such a holding as J.x.x.

Between two five-card suits bid the higher ranking except
when they are spades and clubs, when one club is generally
best. The spades can then be bid and repeated, and the
information that at least ten cards are held in the black suits
can be conveyed at a much lower level than if one spade
is opened.

With three four-card suits, all quite biddable, the one
below the singleton is generally the best to open.

♠ K.Q.x.x	♠ x
♡ x	♡ Q.J.10.x
◇ A.J.x.x	◇ A.K.x.x
♣ A.Q.10.x	♣ K.Q.x.x

Open one diamond on the first hand and one heart on the
second. There is no reason, however, to carry this principle
so far as to open on suits not really biddable.

```
♠ K.10.x.x
♡ A.J.x.x
◇ A.Q.x.x
♣ x
```

It is more sensible to open one heart than to say one
spade in the mistaken belief that the principle stated above
is a ' rule '. You do not really want to finish up in a high
spade contract unless partner can bid the suit as responder.

RANGE OF ONE BIDS

The maximum strength for bids of one is much the
same as in the approach forcing system. If the hand contains a very fine suit, or two good suits, it will be opened
with an Acol two bid, and if the point count is as high as

23 a two club bid is usual. If the count is about 20 or 21 a two no-trump bid is preferred if the hand is evenly distributed, but otherwise an opening bid of one is made. The following hands are all one bids on the system :—

        ♠ A.K.8.6
        ♡ K.Q.J.4
        ♢ 4
        ♣ A.Q.J.3

        ♠ A.J.8.5
        ♡ A.K.J.8.5
        ♢ A.Q.6
        ♣ 4

        ♠ 7
        ♡ K.Q.7.6.4
        ♢ A.Q.8.6.5.3
        ♣ A

None of these hands contains a sufficiently good suit to make a two bid advisable and none of them is of the type of which it can be said that an opening of one may lead to a missed game, or that the bidder will be in difficulties on certain responses.

No-trump bidding is a very exact science in the Acol system. It will be full explained in a later chapter.

CHAPTER III

REBIDS AND RESPONSES

AS the maximum strength for an opening bid of one is much the same as in Culbertson, so is the minimum strength required for partner to respond with on of a suit or with one no-trump. A response is normally given on five points. A suit response is always preferred to one no-trump provided that the suit can be bid at the range of one ; over one heart bid one spade holding :—

In the same way a suit response, even at the level of two, is preferable to the suppression of a six-card suit. Holding :—

the response to a suit bid is two clubs, and not one no-trump.

The minimum for a raise of partner's suit bid is the same as in Culbertson — about $3\frac{1}{2}$ supporting tricks ; in fact all responses at the lower levels are exactly the same as in Culbertson.

NON-FORCING PRINCIPLE

When we come to consider the responses on stronger hands, we encounter one of the fundamental principles of the Acol system and one of the points in which it diverges from modern Culbertson practice. In the

Culbertson system the following responses are forcing to game : A response of two no-trumps : a double raise of the opener's suit.

For Acol players these are limit bids. The two no-trump response denies the ability to bid three, and the double raise denies the values for a triple raise. The bids are not forcing, and the opening bidder may readily pass if he does not fancy the prospects of game. The values for the two no-trump bid are appreciably less than in Culbertson, generally ranging from 11 to 13 points. These hands all demand a response of two no-trumps to a one bid :—

♠ K.10.4
♡ J.7.5
♢ K.10.8.4
♣ K.Q.3

♠ Q.J.6
♡ K.10
♢ A.8.6.4
♣ J.10.5.3

♠ A.J.4
♡ K.Q.8
♢ J.6.4.2
♣ Q.5.3

Only the third of these hands would qualify for a two no-trump response on Culbertson. Hands which are proper two no-trump responses on that system are generally three no-trump bids on Acol. This response suggests a balanced hand containing from 14 to 16 points, but if a player has passed, he may bid three no-trumps on a 13-point hand, so as to show at once that his hand is of maximum strength consistent with a pass.

CHOICE BETWEEN SUIT AND NO-TRUMP RESPONSE

That the point count of a hand is within the limits of a two no-trump or three no-trump response does not

mean that these bids should be made in preference to a
suit call. Three no-trump especially is a response to be
avoided except on hands whose balanced and distributed
strength cannot be shown in any other way.

♠ x.x
♥ A.Q.x.x
♦ x.x.x
♣ A.Q.x.x

Bid two hearts over one spade, avoiding the ragged two
no-trump bid.

♠ Q.x.x
♥ A.J.x.x
♦ K.x
♣ Q.x.x.x

Respond two hearts to one spade mainly because four
spades may be a better contract than three no-trump, and
a two no-trump response is apt to exclude a suit contract
except when partner's hand is unbalanced.

♠ x.x.x.x
♥ A.K.x
♦ A.J.x.x
♣ Q.x

Experience has shown that a slight underbid of three
diamonds over one diamond is the best response. True,
it can be passed, but if partner is strong, to bid three
diamonds makes slam bidding easier than to bid three no-
trump, and if he is weak and has to pass three diamonds,
it may well be that no game contract is possible.

♠ K.x.x
♥ K.x.x.x
♦ A.x
♣ A.Q.x.x

Force with three clubs over any one bid (or with two hearts over one club). The hand is rather too good for three no-trumps, always an unsatisfactory bid when there are slam prospects, although it would be best if the shape were 4-3-3-3. Avoid a simple take-out of two clubs, which is apt to turn out to be a trap bid : for example, the bidding, one diamond, two clubs, two spades, puts the responder in an impossible position. Many players would not hesitate to force on such a hand as this, but there is also a large school of approach forcers who would bid only two clubs ; this style of bidding does not fit in with the Acol system.

THE OPENER'S REBIDS

Not only can the opening bidder pass a two no-trump response if his own hand suggests that the limit has been reached, but he can sign off in his own suit in the confidence that partner will bid again only if his two no-trump bid was a maximum. This is one of the wise measures which are the safeguard of light openings. A player who has opened one spade on :—

♠ K.10.9.8.6.4
♡ A.7.5
◇ Q.3.2
♣ 4

can sign off in three spades, if his partner responds two no-trumps.

Since partner's bid showed the full limit of his hand, it is unlikely that he will bid again ; if he does say four spades, there should be a fair chance of the contract. The corollary of the three-spade sign-off is that the opener should bid four spades himself, if the strength of his hand suggests that that contract should be a make ; he knows that the two no-trump bidder has a minimum of 11 points, and some fit in his suit. Thus if the ace of diamonds were held instead of the queen, four spades should be bid over two no-trumps. A bid in another suit is naturally an inferential force. It is only a minimum rebid of the suit opened which is a sign-off.

A DOUBLE RAISE

The same principle of bidding to the natural limit of the hand applies to raises of partner's suit bid.

The following hands warrant a raise of one spade to three spades :—

♠ Q.J.6.4
♡ 7
◇ K.8.7.6
♣ K.10.8.4

♠ 10.7.6.4.2
♡ 8
◇ A.7.6.3
♣ K.4.2

♠ 7.6.4.3
♡ 8.4
◇ A.Q.6.2
♣ K.Q.3

If the approach forcing system is played, with a double raise forcing, none of these hands is strong enough for three spades, and a simple raise only could be given, or a take-out made into another suit. Acol players obtain a fine result by bidding to the limit ; if partner's opening is light he can pass three spades, and if the contract is defeated it is certain that the opponents have missed a part score if not a game.

Stronger hands, such as would warrant a double raise on Culbertson, are bid to game. Acol players boast that their system is conspicuously free from inhibitions. If a forcing situation is not in being, a player who raises his partner's suit shows the full limit of his hand. The next chapter will show the principles governing the development of the bidding after the opening bid and first response.

CHAPTER IV

LANGUAGE OF BIDS :
MODIFICATION OF THE FORCING PRINCIPLE

THE last chapter laid stress on the natural character of Acol bidding, and showed that such bids as a double raise of partner's suit, and two no-trumps over an opening bid, are not forcing as in Culbertson but are limit bids having natural significance.

Jump bids in a new suit are forcing to game as in all systems, and as already stated a suit response to an opening bid is forcing for one round ; thus one heart over one diamond, or two clubs over one spade, is forcing on the original bidder for one round, a principle now common to all approach forcing and most two club systems. Apart from these bids the Acol system employs none which are by definition forcing but many which are forcing by inference. Some examples will illustrate the distinction between sign-off bids, limit bids, and inferential forces.

South	North
1 ♡	2 N-T
3 ♡	

South's second bid, which on the Culbertson system might be made on a hand of great strength, is in Acol a sign-off. North is supposed to show the full value of his hand by his two no-trump bid ; if South can see game, he is expected to bid it, bidding either three no-trumps or four hearts.

South	North
1 ♢	1 ♡
2 N-T	3 ♡

South's rebid of two no-trumps is not forcing in any rational system, but North's rebid of three hearts would be regarded as an inferential force in Culbertson. For an Acol player the bid would be a sign-off; South has shown 16 to 18 points by his two no-trump bid, and it is up to North to bid the game if he can.

South	North
1 ◇	1 ♡
3 ♡	

South's raise to three hearts expresses the limit of his hand; it is not, as in some systems, a stronger bid than four hearts.

South	North
1 ♡	1 ♠
2 ♣	3 ♡ or 3 ♠

Whether North's second bid is a jump in Spades or in hearts, it is not forcing; South can pass if his hand is weak and game appears improbable. If North can see game in his own hand he must bid it; *remember that Acol players bid their own cards, and don't wait for their partners to bid for them.*

South	North
1 ♠	2 ♣
3 ♠	

South's bid is in no way forcing; the jump rebid is not by definition forcing in the Culbertson system, but it is almost so in practice because of the inadequacy of the system to deal with strong hands.

In the Acol system the jump rebid is freely used on hands worth seven playing tricks; the strength of the bid is always limited by the fact that no use was made of the Acol two opening.

One effect of the frequent use of the jump rebid is the inference that when a minimum rebid of the suit is made, the hand is moderate in strength; in the Culbertson system a simple rebid may conceal quite a good hand, but in Acol the opening cannot be far from a minimum ; *thus is protection afforded to those opening bids which are light in honour strength.*

Many approach forcing players, and especially those who play the losing trick count, are apt to regard a change of suit forcing *ad infinitum*. Acol players have no patience with this theory.

South	North
1 ♡	1 ♠
2 ♣	

North is entirely at liberty to pass this bid if his hand is weak.

A change of suit by the responding hand can equally well be passed by the opening bidder. Here is an example of bidding which earned the players a clear top in a 16-table tournament :—

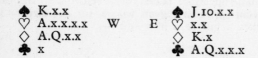

♠ K.x.x   ♠ J.10.x.x
♡ A.x.x.x.x   W   E   ♡ x.x
♢ A.Q.x.x   ♢ K.x
♣ x   ♣ A.Q.x.x.x

The bidding was :—

West	East
1 ♡	2 ♣
2 ♢	2 ♠
No bid	

Nine tricks were made at the spade contract ; at all other tables E-W floundered in two no-trumps or some other unmakeable contract.

From the bidding situations given it will be realised that one of the fundamental principles of the Acol system is that where no forcing situation is in being a player can

always pass ; he never has to bid his partner's cards for
him. The advantage of this principle is that Acol players
have every chance of finding the contract which best suits
their combined hands ; with hands of moderate strength
they are never afflicted with the bogy that they dare not
show their distribution because a change of suit is a sign
of considerable strength. The corollary to this argument is
that neither opener nor responder should fail to produce a
secondary force when not prepared for the bidding to die
short of game.

INFERENTIAL FORCES

Notwithstanding the principle enunciated in the last
section, that a player need never bid his partner's cards,
Acol players make use of a highly developed system of
inferential forces. There are a great many bidding situations
(distinct from those given so far in this chapter), in which
the inferences which can be deduced from the bids already
made, are such that it is inconceivable that the bidding should
die without at least one further bid. At the same time no
forcing bid, properly so called, has been made. An obvious
example occurs when a player, whose suit has already been
raised, makes a bid in a new suit :—

However weak his raise North should bid three spades.
South has heard his partner make the rather weak response
of two spades, and by continuing the bidding he more or
less guarantees that three spades at least is safe. His three
club bid is an experimental bid—in modern parlance a
trial bid ; probably he is bidding three clubs in order to
test whether his partner can now show that his raise was a
fair one and bid four spades ; in other words, North should
read the three club bid as equivalent to three-and-a-half
spades, and should respond three spades or four spades
according to the worth of his hand.

Another situation which amounts to an inferential force arises from this bidding :—

South	North
1 ♣	2 ♦
3 ♣	

North should not pass ; South has shown a good hand, since he has carried the bidding to the range of three despite the possibility of North having a weak response ; had his hand been other than good, his rebid would have been two spades, instead of three clubs ; alternatively he would have opened one club. In default of a better bid North should say three diamonds, which affirms no more than that he holds a fair diamond suit.

Another bidding sequence which should not be dropped is this :—

1 ♠	2 ♦
2 ♡	3 ♣

Had the opener rebid two spades, however, a minimum in his own suit, three clubs would not have been forcing, and responder would have to bid four clubs if determined to reach game.

Many inferential forces are too obvious to require comment. For example, the bidding :—

South	North
1 ♠	2 N-T
3 ♡	

This clearly does not permit of a pass by North. Rather less obvious are the inferences conveyed by the following auction :—

South	North
1 ♠	2 ♦
2 N-T	3 ♣

This last bid by North is an inferential force ; had North held a moderate hand, with a diamond suit and support for spades such as :—

♠ K.8.4
♡ 7.6
◇ A.10.8.5.3
♣ 8.7.4

his first response should have been two spades. It is an established principle for all good bidders that when a hand is worth only one bid, preference should be given to a raise of partner's suit. In the present example, therefore, North is marked with a good hand, and he is simply offering South a choice between three no-trumps and four spades.

Provided that the cardinal principles of Acol bidding are borne in mind, it is not difficult to reason out the implications of any bidding situation which may arise.

CHAPTER V

NO-TRUMP BIDS AND RESPONSES

*T*HERE *is no department in the Acol System which is more strictly standardised than no-trump bids and responses. The theories advocated represent a logical extension of the principles explained in Culbertson's* Gold Book.

The opening bid of one no-trump is the only bid in the system which is substantially affected by the vulnerability position. There is a very sound reason why a vulnerable no-trump should not be bid on anything but a powerful hand ; it is that the danger of a double and a pass by the doubler's partner is very great, and the penalty that can ensue if the dummy hand is worthless outweighs the advantage of opening with a light no-trump. The point count, used by all Acol players, of 4 for an ace, 3 for a king, 2 for a queen, and 1 for a jack, plays a prominent part in no-trump bidding. To bid one no-trump not vulnerable, the hand should be worth about a king above the average ; if vulnerable, at least two kings above the average. In terms of the point count, the limits are as follows :—

For a non-vulnerable no-trump, 13 to 15 points.

For a vulnerable no-trump, 16 to 18 points.

So exact are the responses to no-trump bids that it is unwise to stray beyond the limits indicated ; these are so precise that when a hand conforms to the point count requirements, and is of a balanced pattern, either 4-3-3-3, 4-4-3-2, or even 5-3-3-2 (when the five-card suit is a minor), the fact that a biddable suit is held should not, as in some systems, exclude a no-trump bid. At the same time, it is a bad habit to open one no-trump on hands that obviously may well play better in a suit call.

♠ K.10
♡ K.J.8
◇ A.J.5.3
♣ Q.9.6.4

Count, 14 points.

If a player were vulnerable, he would call one diamond on this hand, but if not vulnerable, he has an excellent no-trump bid.

♠ A.Q.4
♡ A.Q.6.5
◇ J.8.5
♣ K.J.10

Count, 17 points.

This is too strong for a bid of one no-trump not vulnerable, and the bid is one heart; if vulnerable, the player should choose the bid which gives the best picture of this hand, one no-trump.

RESPONSES TO BIDS OF ONE NO-TRUMP

In respect of opening no-trump bids Acol players follow principles which are common to many systems. For responses they employ natural methods now common to all good systems. A new bid is being tried out, but it is not yet part of the system, so it is discussed separately in a later chapter.

So precise are the limits of opening no-trump bids that the responder is supposed to be able to judge at once what is likely to be the best final contract; the corollary of this principle is that the no-trump bidder is not supposed to repeat himself.

This does not mean that a player who has opened one no-trump must hold his peace ever after, unless partner forces, but that he is not expected to rebid his hand except for a very good reason. A raise to two no-trumps always constitutes a good reason for the opening bidder to call game. Since the limit of the opening bid if 13 to 15 points not vulnerable, the partner can bid three no-trumps on 12 points, should raise to two no-trumps on 10 or 11, and should pass on less, unless his hand is strengthened by a five-card suit or is fitted for a suit take out.

If the player is vulnerable a raise to two no-trumps should be given on 7 or 8 points and to three no-trumps on 9 points. In all cases allowance should be made for strong intermediates and for long suits.

♠ K.10.6.4.3
♥ J.6
♦ Q.10.8
♣ K.9.4

Count, 9 points.

The hand is one point short for a raise to two no-trumps not vulnerable, but the five-card suit makes the raise worth while. Vulnerable, three no-trumps should be bid ; it would be a mistake to bid the spades, as the hand is likely to make the same number of tricks in spades and in no-trumps.

♠ K.7
♥ 8.4
♦ A.10.9.6.4.2
♣ 10.5.4

Count, 7 points.

Not vulnerable, make a simple take-out into two diamonds ; vulnerable, the choice is between two diamonds and three no-trumps ; the latter bid is the right shot; it is unintelligent to adopt the compromise of two no-trumps, for if this is to be passed, better be in two diamonds.

A player who has opened one no-trump and been raised to two no-trumps should bid game unless his opening was a minimum. Suppose, for example, a player has 14 points and his not vulnerable no-trump bid is raised to two no-trumps; partner has 10 or 11 points; the minimum combined count is therefore 24, which, unless there is a conspicuous absence of good intermediates and suit lengths, just makes the game worth bidding.

The effect of this system is that Acol players very seldom end up in the obviously unsatisfactory contract of two no-trumps; and when they do, they generally have 23 points between them, or a barren 24, and two no-trumps is exactly what they make.

If you take the trouble to work out every possible situation, you will see that when the opening bid has been one no-trump a pair can never reach three no-trumps on *less* than 24 points (unless there is great suit length), and can never be out of three no-trumps on *more* than 24 points.

THE TAKE-OUT INTO TWO OF A SUIT

The Acol theory of no-trump raises makes it possible to rescue bids of one no-trump into two of a suit. You hold :—

♠ 10.7.6.4.3.2
♡ 8
♢ Q.6.4.3
♣ 5.4

Partner opens one no-trump and second hand passes; vulnerable or not you can bid two spades without the

awful fear, present in some systems, that partner will bid
two no-trumps or even three no-trumps; in nine cases
out of ten he will pass; very occasionally, if his no-trump
bid was a maximum, and he has a fine fit for spades, he
will bid three spades — never four.

♠ J
♡ 10.7.6.3
♢ A.K.6.4.2
♣ 7.6.4

Not vulnerable you rescue into two diamonds;
vulnerable, bid two no-trumps; remember that partner
will pass two diamonds, thinking that there is no play
for game — that is what your bid has told him!

THE TAKE-OUT INTO THREE OF A SUIT

A jump take-out into three of a suit is forcing to game
but does not indicate great strength; it simply shows that
the responder, having in view the known strength of his
partner's hand, visualises a game and is undecided whether
to play in no-trumps or a suit.

♠ K.10.8.6.4
♡ 8
♢ A.9.4.2
♣ J.5.3

Not vulnerable, take out into two spades—the best
contract for the combined hands. Vulnerable, bid three
spades, and pass if partner says three no-trumps.

THE REBID FOLLOWING A JUMP TAKE-OUT

The opening bidder whose partner has made a jump
take-out, should bear in mind that his partner's bid suggests

an unbalanced hand. In the majority of cases, therefore, his rebid should be a raise of the suit, and not three no-trumps, which is correct only if a doubleton of the suit is held, or a 4-3-3-3 pattern particularly well suited to no-trump play.

♠ A.7.6
♡ K.9.4
♢ A.Q.8.3
♣ A.10.4

Partner bids three spades over your vulnerable no-trump bid ; avoid the common mistake of bidding three no-trumps ; partner has shown an unbalanced hand by his response, and your hand will play well in spades, and may be unsafe in no-trumps, through its comparative paucity of honour cards, and fear of a menace suit being readily established. Bid four spades.

THE TAKE-OUT INTO THREE CLUBS

The partner of a no-trump bidder sometimes would prefer to find a major suit contract if his partner has four cards of it. In this situation he should bid three clubs and it is then incumbent upon the no-trump bidder to bid a major if he has four cards of it.

♠ K.5.2			♠ Q.J.9.4
♡ Q.5.4.2	W	E	♡ A.J.10.6
♢ K.7.6			♢ 4.2
♣ A.Q.8			♣ K.5.2

West bids one no-trump not vulnerable and East bids three clubs ; West must now say three hearts and so the best contract is found.

In this example the responder had both major suits, but the convention is equally valuable if only one is held.

♠ x
♡ K.J.x.x
◇ A.x.x.x
♣ K.J.10.x

Here again three clubs should be bid over one no-trump ; if partner can say three hearts, so much the better ; if not, three no-trumps will be passed, but at least the attempt has been made to find the safest spot.

STRONGER NO-TRUMP BIDS

An opening bid of two no-trumps shows 20 to 21 points, and occasionally the bid is made on 22. From these premises it is easy for the responding hand to judge what is his best line of action. A take-out into three of a suit is an inferential force as in all systems and might be made equally on a weak hand and a very strong one. A bid of four in a major suit does not show a long, weak suit, which can be indicated by minimum rebids, but is a mild slam invitation.

♠ K.Q.7.6.4.2
♡ K.6
◇ J.4
♣ 7.5.3

Bid four spades over two no-trumps, inviting partner to bid a slam, if his hand is rich in honour tricks and controls.

Very powerful hands, containing 23 points or more, are dealt with by means of the Acol two club bid, and will be discussed in connection with it.

SUMMARY OF THE ACOL NO-TRUMP THEORY

The underlying principle of no-trump bidding is one which is common to all Acol bidding :—" Bid your own cards to the limit, and don't expect partner to bid them for you ; partner will not repeat himself, when he has shown the exact character of his hand."

CHAPTER VI

THE ACOL TWO BID (1)

*I*N this chapter is presented the pivotal bid in the Acol
System, the bid which distinguishes it from all other
systems.

*The Acol two bid is used on hands of power and quality,
whose strength is not fully expressed by an opening bid of one
and a jump rebid. Negatively, the use of the Acol two bid
facilitates the whole system of constructive bidding, by narrowing
the range of hands which have to be opened with a bid of one.*

Through the absence of conventional forcing bids in the
Culbertson system, the range of hands which are opened
with a bid of one is excessively wide. The result of this is
that hands of too greatly varying strength have to be bid
in the same way, either through a simple rebid or a jump
rebid. This difficulty does not exist for orthodox one club
and two club systems, but the qualities which are the especial
recommendation of the approach forcing method are absent
from these systems. The greatest merit of the Culbertson
system is the varied character of the opening bid of one,
which carries with it all the advantages of surprise, adapta-
bility, and simplicity, which are the characteristics of the
ideal bid. The principal defect of the two club systems is
that a bid of one is limited to hands of moderate strength,
and a bid of two is essential on hands which for their development require time and the maximum interchange of
information ; those very hands, which demand the highest
degree of constructive bidding, have to be opened, simply
because they are strong, at an unnecessarily high range.

The Acol system retains all the virtues of the Culbertson
system, while overcoming its greatest weakness—inadequate

machinery to deal with strong hands. It has three bids at its disposal for these hands, a bid of one, a two club bid, and a bid of two in another suit. The function of these bids can quite simply be explained.

The Acol two club bid is (with one minor exception) forcing to game, and is not made on less than five honour tricks.

The Acol two bid, two spades, two hearts, or two diamonds, is reserved for hands containing not fewer than eight playing tricks, and at least one powerful suit ; there is no specified honour trick content. The bid is forcing for one round.

A bid of one may be made on a hand containing as many as six honour tricks, if the distribution and playing strength are such that it cannot be regarded as a game hand.

EXAMPLES OF ACOL TWO BIDS

There follows a list of some of the considerations which persuade a player to open with an Acol two bid ; as a rule, where one of the reasons exists, so does another.

1.   The hand is of the type which, if opened with a bid of one, will be difficult to bid exactly in the event of certain responses ; in other words a bid of one may turn out to be a trap bid. Example :—

♠ A.K.Q.J.x.x
♥ A.x.x
&diamonds; A.x.x
♣ x

Suppose you open one spade, as on Culbertson you must ; partner responds two hearts or two diamonds ; now can you find a bid which does not risk missing a slam, or jeopardising a game ?

2.   The hand is a powerful two suiter. Example :—

♠ A.Q.J.x.x.x
♡ K.Q.J.x.x.x
♢ x
♣ None

Rather an anxious hand for Culbertson bidders, whether they decide to open with a bid of one or a bid of two ; if they bid one spade, there is a slight fear that the hand will be passed out, and if it is not, there is sure to be a difficulty in showing partner the character of the hand ; if they open two spades, there is a constant danger lest partner, misled as to the honour trick strength of the hand, will carry the bidding too high, the contract being ruined through duplication of values.

3.   The hand is top-heavy.

♠ A.Q.J.9.8.7.6.4
♡ 7
♢ A.J.4
♣ 5

Not an easy hand to bid on any system, and quite impossible on most. The Acol player, by opening two spades, and bidding three spades over any response, presents as good a picture of the hand as is possible—eight or nine playing tricks in spades, sufficient power to make a preemptive bid of four spades unnecessary, and no second suit ; if partner has a blank hand, three spades is the final contract, if the opponents do not bid. If a player opens with a bid of one spade, he must bid four on the next round, without any certainty that he has found the best contract.

4.   The hand is so powerful that, for game to be a lay-down, partner requires to hold a certain card, which will not entitle him to respond to a bid of one.

♠ K.Q.x.x
♡ A.K.J.10.x.x.x
◇ K.x
♣ None

An awkward hand both for Culbertson bidders and orthodox two club bidders. One hardly cares to open with a bid which is not forcing to game, since partner requires to have only the knave of spades to make the game almost a certainty ; on the other hand, the honour trick strength does not justify a two club bid on the system. Acol players have no difficulty ; they open two hearts, and if partner bids two no-trumps, they say three hearts ; partner will raise to four, if his hand contains values even so slight that he could not keep open a one bid.

5. Hands containing about nine playing tricks in diamonds.

♠ A
♡ K.x.x
◇ A.J.10.9.x.x.x.x.x
♣ None

A nightmare hand for any but an Acol bidder, who opens two diamonds, and rebids the suit without animation until partner produces a blessed heart bid.

6. A hand which, although it contains no very powerful suit, such as normally recommends an Acol two bid, is of the general strength which makes it too strong for a bid of one and not strong enough for a bid unconditionally forcing to game. The two hands which follow were held by North and South in two matches played in a League contest ; the same hands were used for both matches, so that four sets of bidding can be compared.

♠ A.5
♡ K.Q.6.3
♢ A.K.Q.8.4
♣ A.J

       N

       S

♠ J.7.6.2
♡ 10.8.5.4.2
♢ 7.6
♣ 9.5

North was the dealer, and his side was vulnerable ; the opponents did not bid at any table. These were the results :—

1. North and South were playing Culbertson : North opened one diamond, fearing to force on a hand which is not quite of game-going strength. South passed, and the hand was played in one diamond.

2. North, playing the Lederer two club system, opened two clubs ; South bid two diamonds. North said three diamonds, and not regarding the bid as forcing, South passed, afraid to mention his hearts ; had he done so his partner would undoubtedly have raised him above the game level.

3. Playing the official two club, forcing to game, North bid two clubs ; South said two diamonds, and North two no-trumps ; South bid three hearts, and North raised him to five hearts ; he can hardly do less ; the contract was one down.

4. At this table, playing Acol, North, so far from being in difficulties on the hand, had a choice of bidding methods, both absolutely safe. He could bid two clubs, and over two diamonds make the non-forcing rebid of two no-trumps ; then South would bid three hearts, and North, having

already shown tremendous power, would not need to bid more than four hearts. Alternatively, he could bid two diamonds, and over two no-trumps three hearts ; if partner's hand was blank, the hand would be played in three hearts. He chose this method, and over three hearts South bid four hearts. Thus at only one table in four was this seemingly simple game bid and made.

THE BORDER-LINE FOR TWO BIDS

It is just as important to know when a hand is under strength for a two bid as to recognise the occasion for its proper use. Players accustomed to the theory of ordinary two club systems find it difficult to follow the part played by two bids in the Acol system, so that the following examples should be studied with care.

♠ A.K.6.4.2
♡ A.Q.8.5.3
◇ A
♣ 6.2

Now this is a useful hand but it lacks the concentrated strength which one associates with an Acol two bid. Note that it presents no difficulty if bid on ordinary approach forcing lines ; one spade is opened and a force of three hearts made on the next round. To make the hand a proper two bid, the suits should be strengthened somewhat ; the queen of spades instead of a small one, or the two major suit jacks, would just about turn the scale.

♠ A.J.7.6.5.3
♡ 4
◇ A.K.2
♣ A.Q.5

This hand again is just below standard. When in doubt, remember that the best test is to ask oneself whether a bid of one is likely to turn out to be a trap bid in the event of certain responses. Let us say that over one spade partner says two diamonds or two clubs ; declarer must find a forcing bid in the other minor suit and reach game in spades or another suit, depending on partner's later bidding. The hand would be a proper two bid if either (1) the spades were strengthened to something like A.Q.10.9.x.x, or (2) a seventh spade were added in place of any small card, or (3) the king of clubs were introduced in place of the queen. The last change would not make the hand by any means an ideal two bid, but on the whole it would be correct so to open. Observe that if one spade is opened on :

    ♠   A.J.7.6.5.3
    ♡   4
    ♢   A.K.2
    ♣   A.K.5

and partner responds with a bid of two in a minor suit, the bidding is most tricky. The Acol two bid is used on hands of power and quality, and the fine quality of the hand above, reflected in its five honour tricks, compensates for the fact that in power it is slightly below standard.

One point about the Acol two bid cannot fail to have struck the discriminating reader ; it is that, whereas in the ordinary two club systems, the two bid is apt to lose time, the Acol two bid almost always saves time. By indicating at one stroke the great playing strength of the hand, it removes the necessity for an excessively high jump rebid.

The next chapter will show how the subsequent bidding is developed.

CHAPTER VII

THE ACOL TWO BID (2)

*S*O *exact is the meaning of an Acol two bid, and so sure the guarantee that strong playing values are held, that the responder can bid his cards in the most natural way, without fear that he is imposing a strain upon his partner. So much is said by the opening bid, that there is ample time thereafter to explore all the possibilities of the combined hands. In other systems precious time may be wasted in high jump rebids by the opening hand; in the Acol system all this information is given in the opening bid, and the auction can then develop at leisure.*

The character of the Acol two bid has been explained in full, and no one who has read the last chapter should make the mistake of thinking that Acol is simply a system which opens fair hands with a bid of one, better ones with a bid of two, and the best with a two club bid. The Acol two bid is reserved for hands of a type, and not for hands of any special degree of general strength. The hands which require time for their development are opened with the bid which allows most time, a bid of one.

RESPONSES TO THE ACOL TWO BID

The weakness response is two no-trumps. If the responder's hand is blank, containing neither distributional nor honour values, he can pass the opener's rebid, unless it is a jump rebid in a new suit. With very slight supporting values, however, he should find a bid, especially if his partner indicates a two-suited hand.

♠ Q.x.x
♡ x.x.x.x
◇ x.x
♣ J.x.x.x

If partner opens two spades, you bid two no-trumps, and
if he then bids three spades, you should raise to four.
Remember that he may well have opened with a bid of two,
because he could see a prospect of game, even though you
might have to pass a one bid. He is known to have at least
eight playing tricks in spades ; your queen must be worth
one trick ; your doubleton in diamonds may provide a
ruffing trick and, if not, perhaps your club jack will come
in useful.

♠ x.x
♡ Q.10.x
◇ x.x.x.x
♣ x.x.x.x

If partner opens two spades, and rebids three spades
over your two no-trumps, you will naturally pass ; but if
his rebid is three hearts, you should give him four, as your
doubleton in his first suit, together with your honour in
his second, is sure to be worth a trick or two.

♠ x.x
♡ K.10.x
◇ Q.J.x.x
♣ 10.x.x.x

Over two spades you say two no-trumps, and if partner
rebids three spades, you should say three no-trumps ;
partner will realise from this that you have a little scattered
strength, and will either bid four spades, or pass, in the
assurance that you have a guard in a couple of suits. If
partner rebids three in another suit, you should raise that

suit ; reflect that partner has a two-suiter, and is not interested in no-trumps ; it will be of much greater interest to him to know that you can support his second suit.

RAISING PARTNER'S SUIT

A simple raise of an Acol two bid is a two-way bid, as is the simple raise of a forcing two bid in the Culbertson system. It may signify a weak hand, containing support for the suit bid, and about one honour trick, or it may be that the responding hand is strong, intends to take further action, and is simply agreeing the suit for the present.

♠ x.x.x
♡ K.x.x
◇ A.x.x.x
♣ J.x.x

Raise two hearts to three hearts. If partner simply bids four hearts, you will pass ; if he takes stronger action, he can be marked with a very powerful hand, and you can show your diamond ace.

A simple raise is equally correct on the South hand in the following example of a freak hand from America, which was quoted to show the value of asking bids.

♠ K.Q.x.x.x.x
♡ A.K.J.10.x.x.x
◇ Nil
♣ Nil

N

S

♠ A.x
♡ Q.9.x.x
◇ A.x.x
♣ J.x.x.x

North, playing Acol, would open two hearts. South's response is three hearts ; if North responds four hearts, South intends to cue bid his spade ace, giving North a chance to bid four no-trumps, to which he can bid five no-trumps. As it is, North says three spades. South bids four diamonds, showing the ace ; had South held a diamond suit he would have shown it with his first response. North now bids four spades, presenting a fine picture of his hand ; despite the fact that hearts have been supported, he has twice bid another suit, so he is marked with a complete two-suiter ; South says five spades, which North reads as showing the ace, and so he bids the grand slam in hearts.

THE DOUBLE RAISE

A double raise of an Acol two bid is a very exact response. Since it is generally correct to give a single raise on a hand containing trump support and one or more aces, a double raise is reserved for hands containing exceptionally good trump support, a certain amount of high card strength, and no aces.

      ♠ K.8.6.4
      ♡ Q.J.9.3
      ◇ 4
      ♣ K.7.5.2

A bid of two spades or two hearts should be raised to four ; partner is immediately informed that you have four trumps, some distributional values, a few high cards, but no aces. Don't make the mistake of producing this double raise simply on the strength of good trump support. If the hand is generally moderate, two no-trumps should be the first response if there is less than one honour trick, and a single raise given if there is an honour trick or more. The double raise is designed for good, but ace-less, hands which suggest the need for an effort in the direction of slam, but have no primary control in which the effort can be made.

A RESPONSE IN A NEW SUIT

No precise standard is laid down for a positive response to an Acol two bid, any more than it is for a positive response to a Culbertson two bid. If a biddable suit is held, which can be bid at the range of two, one honour trick suffices ; if the suit has to be bid at the range of three, the hand should normally contain one and a half honour tricks.

When as good support as Q.x.x is held in partner's suit, it is generally better to raise the suit than to bid a moderate suit of one's own.

♠ Q.x.x
♡ A.J.10.x
♢ x.x
♣ K.x.x.x

Bid two hearts over two diamonds, but three spades over two spades.

A SUIT BID AFTER A TWO NO-TRUMP RESPONSE

The significance of a subsequent suit call by a responder who on the first round has said two no-trumps, depends upon the method of bidding followed by the opener.

(1) If the opener rebids his own suit at a minimum level, responder may show any fair holding which he thinks may fill a gap in partner's hand for no-trump, or may serve as the best final contract.

♠ Q.J.8.6.4
♡ 10.7.2
♢ 6.3
♣ Q.4.2

If the bidding is two hearts, two no-trump by this hand, three hearts, responder should simply bid four hearts. If partner opens and rebids diamonds, three spades can be bid on the second round. Partner may have three to an honour and four spades be the best contract : alternatively, the bid may enable partner to bid three no-trump.

(2) If the opener rebids in a new suit over two no-trump, responder should *not* show a moderate holding of another suit. The logic of this distinction is that, since partner has shown a two-suiter, he is not likely to be interested in no-trumps and he is not likely to have something like K.x.x in this third suit. Therefore, after partner has shown a two-suiter, only a very good suit is worth mentioning, one so good that the responder wishes it to be trumps even though partner has shown two good suits of his own.

♠ Nil   ♠ K.J.10.9.6.5.4
♡ A.K.J.8.5.2   W   E   ♡ 3
◇ K.Q.J.9.3   ◇ 5.2
♣ K.10   ♣ 8.6.4

The bidding should be :—

West	East
2 ♡	2 N-T
3 ◇	3 ♠
No bid	

When East bids three spades, West should realise the character of his hand and should have the self-discipline to give up.

A RESPONSE OF THREE NO-TRUMPS

When the responding hand contains a fair amount of strength and no biddable suit, a response of three no-trumps is in order.

♠ x.x
♡ K.10.x.x
◇ A.J.x
♣ K.9.x.x

Over two spades bid three no-trumps.

REBIDS BY THE OPENING BIDDER

A player who has opened with an Acol two bid seldom has any difficulty in the subsequent bidding. If partner signs off with two no-trumps, and the opener has a hand so strong that he can make game even though partner holds a Yarborough, he should bid game himself. With a gigantic two-suiter it is, about once in six months, necessary to make a jump bid in the second suit.

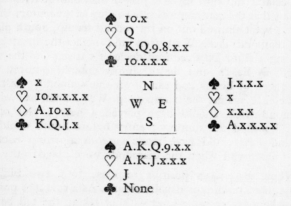

```
                    ♠ 10.x
                    ♡ Q
                    ◇ K.Q.9.8.x.x
                    ♣ 10.x.x.x
♠ x                ┌─────────┐        ♠ J.x.x.x
♡ 10.x.x.x.x.x     │    N    │        ♡ x
◇ A.10.x           │  W   E  │        ◇ x.x.x
♣ K.Q.J.x          │    S    │        ♣ A.x.x.x.x
                   └─────────┘
                    ♠ A.K.Q.9.x.x
                    ♡ A.K.J.x.x.x
                    ◇ J
                    ♣ None
```

There is something to be said for opening two clubs on South's hand, but it is better to open two spades, with the intention of bidding four hearts over a negative response. When the hand was played, South opened two spades and North responded three diamonds. There was no point, after this response, in bidding four hearts, so South bid three hearts and was given preference to three spades. South bid four no-trumps and North signed off with five diamonds. This meant that an ace was missing, so the bidding closed at six spades.

West opened the king of clubs and South ruffed. If the jack of diamonds is played at trick 2, West has a difficult decision whether or not to take the trick. If West holds off, the right continuation for declarer is to play a heart to the queen, a spade to the ace and then a small heart, trumping with dummy's spade ten. This safety play takes care of the distribution which actually existed—a singleton heart and four spades to the jack held by one defender. Actually West should win the trick if a diamond is led in trick 2. Then it is imperative that he should play a heart, for the situation is the same as that which arose in actual play.

Declarer did not, in fact, play a diamond at trick 2, for he saw that the contract was safe so long as the trumps broke. When West showed out on the second trump, South played the diamond jack. West won and made the mistake of playing a club. This reduced declarer's trumps to the same length as East's, and South simply entered dummy with the queen of hearts and ran down the diamonds. East had no defence against the trump coup. West, when he won the diamond trick, should have played a heart; this would have knocked out dummy's entry before South could use it, and East could have made sure of a trump trick by refusing to ruff when the diamonds were played out.

When there is a positive response to a two bid, the subsequent bidding is usually simple. As a rule it is possible to make a try of some kind without taking the bid beyond the game level.

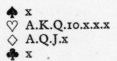

♠ x
♡ A.K.Q.10.x.x.x
♢ A.Q.J.x
♣ x

If over two hearts partner bids two no-trumps, you should bid four hearts ; if he bids spades or clubs, it is well to rebid hearts before showing diamonds ; if he raises to three hearts, you bid four diamonds, and if this fails to excite, you will know that he does not hold the diamond king and an ace, and will accordingly pass his bid of four hearts. Some examples of slam bidding following an Acol two bid are given in Chapter X.

CHAPTER VIII

THE ACOL TWO CLUB

THE *Acol two club bid works very simply, and differs little from the two club bid of other systems. The non-forcing character of a rebid of two no-trumps makes it possible for the partners to stay out of those awkward three no-trump contracts which occur when one hand has what, in other systems, is a three no-trump bid, and the dummy is completely worthless.*

An opening bid of two clubs is an artificial bid in the Acol system, and is forcing to game, with the one exception that the responder may pass a blank hand if the opener rebids two no-trumps. A holding of five or more honour tricks is guaranteed by the two club bidder ; if the hand is of game-going strength, but does not contain five quick tricks, it is opened with an Acol two bid. The following examples will show clearly the use of the two club bid :—

♠ A.K.x.x
♥ x
♦ A.Q.J.x
♣ A.K.x.x

This hand contains five and a half honour tricks, but it no more demands a game-forcing bid in the Acol system than it does in the Culbertson system. Open one diamond, choosing the suit below the singleton, in order to facilitate the course of the bidding in the event of a heart response.

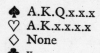

♠ A.K.Q.x.x.x
♥ A.K.x.x.x.x
♦ None
♣ x

Although this is a certain game hand, two clubs should not be called in case partner, holding the A.K of diamonds and the king of clubs, should assume that the opening bidder must hold the club ace in order to make up his five quick tricks. The way to bid this hand is to open two spades, and if the response is a negative two no-trumps, say four hearts.

♠ A.Q.x
♡ K.J.x
♢ A.Q.J.x
♣ A.K.x

This hand contains a 24 count and is of the type which demands a two club opening, followed by a bid of two no-trumps over the weakness response of two diamonds. If this bid is passed, partner holding less than 3 points, it is unlikely that you will make nine tricks.

The non-forcing character of the two no-trump rebid makes it possible to stay out of a game when one player holds a colossal hand and the other a nearly blank hand. The two club opening, followed by a two no-trump rebid, shows 23 points, and partner should raise to game on one king, or a queen and a jack.

♠ A.x
♡ K.Q.x
♢ A.K.Q.10.x
♣ A.x.x

This hand contains only 22 points, but the strong diamond suit makes it a sound two club bid to be followed by a two no-trump rebid. Most players, playing approach forcing, would open three no-trump on the hand, but at Acol there is no need for the slight gamble.

A REBID TO THREE NO-TRUMPS

A balanced hand, containing 26 points or more, should be opened with a bid of two clubs, and three no-trumps bid on the next round.

AN ORIGINAL THREE NO-TRUMP BID

Since a genuine three no-trump hand is preceded by a bid of two clubs, it follows that when an Acol player opens with a bid of three no-trumps, there is something funny about the hand. The meaning of the original three no-trump bid is usually that the player who makes it thinks he has a reasonable chance of making the contract, provided he is left to play in three no-trumps ; he does not want to be rescued into a suit call.

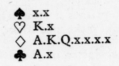

♠ x.x
♡ K.x
◇ A.K.Q.x.x.x.x
♣ A.x

This is a reasonable opening three no-trump bid ; by opening with this bid, the player ensures that his partner, holding something like six spades to the ten, will not rescue him into four spades.

It is interesting to observe the extraordinary accuracy with which strong hands can be bid in the Acol two club bid. Where the forcing two system has two bids for strong, balanced hands, two no-trumps and three no-trumps, the Acol system has four ways of bidding.

1.   *An opening bid of two no-trumps shows 20 to 22 points.*

2.   *An opening bid of two clubs, followed by a bid of two no-trumps, shows 23 to 25 points.*

3.   *An opening bid of two clubs, followed by a bid of three no-trumps, shows 26 points or more.*

4. *An opening bid of three no-trumps shows probably about eight tricks, and a desire to play the hand in that contract.*

RESPONDING TO A TWO CLUB BID

For a positive response to a two club bid any one of the following combinations is needed : an ace and a king ; four kings ; a K.Q and two kings ; two K.Q.s ; if none of these combinations is held, the bid is two diamonds. However weak the hand, the bidding cannot be dropped short of game unless the opener rebids two no-trumps, when the responder can pass if he holds less than 3 points. If the requirements for a positive response are held, the player should respond in any biddable suit, and if he has none, he should bid two no-trumps. Having given a negative reply, the responder is free to bid a suit on the next round, even if his hand is very weak. Here is an example from a pairs event :—

♠ A.Q.x
♡ A.K.Q.x
◇ x
♣ A.K.Q.10.x

N

S

♠ x.x.x
♡ x.x
◇ Q.J.x.x.x
♣ x.x.x

Almost every pair reached five clubs on this hand, and went down. The Acol bidding was very simple : North opened two clubs, and over two diamonds bid two hearts, preferring to make a bid at the range of two, rather than say three clubs. South confidently bid three diamonds, and

so the bidding closed at three no-trumps, while at other
tables South did not show his diamond strength in time.

A jump bid in no-trumps is often the correct bid for the
responding hand.

♠ x.x.x
♡ A.J.x
◇ Q.10.x
♣ Q.x.x.x

If the bidding is two clubs, two diamonds, two spades,
the responder should now bid three no-trumps, showing
that, although he had not an ace and a king for a positive
response, his hand nevertheless contains some high cards.

When a player has opened with a bid of two clubs, his
hand is known to be exceptionally powerful, and inexperienced players may have difficulty in valuing their hands
in support.

♠ J.x
♡ A.10.x
◇ Q.J.x.x.x
♣ x.x.x

Partner opens two clubs, and you say two diamonds, not
having an ace and a king. Partner now says two spades, and
you three diamonds. Now if partner says three no-trumps,
you must not imagine that you have done your bit in saying
three diamonds ; you must say four no-trumps, showing
that you have a useful hand in support of a two club bid
and giving partner a chance to bid on.

A JUMP BID IN A FORCING SITUATION

It is convenient to mention at this point that throughout
the Acol system a jump bid made when a forcing situation

is in being shows a suit with at least six tricks and in all probability no losers : the suit should be as good as A.K.Q.J.x.x or seven to the A.K.Q. The bid is useful when the auction proceeds in this way :—

North	South
1 ♠	3 ◇
4 ♠	

By making the jump rebid when three spades could not be passed, the opener shows that his suit requires no support, information which may be of great value to responder.

When this bid is made by a player who has opened two clubs, it not only shows the solid suit, but proclaims that he is taking charge of the bidding and is interested exclusively in aces.

North	South
2 ♣	2 ◇
3 ♡	

Now South must bid any ace which he holds : he may indicate a void only if he has a fair holding in trumps. If he has no aces or void, he says three no-trumps. If after this three no-trump bid the opener makes a call in a suit other than hearts, an exceptional situation is reached demanding special treatment. There is no occasion for a fixed schedule of bids by the responding hand, but it is running little risk of infection from the asking bug to say that responder should obviously raise this suit if he has the king of it. Note that these bidding methods proceed from the logic of the situation. Anything in the nature of artificial asking bids is foreign to the Acol outlook, and it is the contention of Acol bidders that when specific information is required, it can usually be obtained by intelligent use of the natural resources of the system.

c

The jump bid to show a solid suit should also be made by the responder to a two bid or two club bid, if he is so fortunate as to have the requirements for it. If in either case the jump is made after a negative response has been given on the previous round, then naturally it has a different meaning, simply showing a very long suit and little high card value.

CHAPTER IX

PRE-EMPTIVE BIDS — ATTACK AND DEFENCE

THE Acol system is so well equipped with bids for strong hands that, as may be imagined, an opening three bid is pre-emptive in character. In the first year of the system an extremely weak three bid was played, but in recent years there has been a tendency to make the bids slightly stronger.

The requirements are about six playing tricks when not vulnerable, and seven playing tricks when vulnerable. The opponents' score should also be taken into account ; position at the table is another important factor ; third hand is the most favourable position for a weak bid, especially when not vulnerable against vulnerable opponents, and first hand is better suited to a pre-emptive bid than second hand.

A fourth hand three bid is a rarity, for which the occasion arises now and then at match point play ; it suggests about seven playing tricks, and an expectation of making the contract, if partner has his fair share of the outstanding cards.

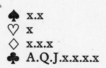

This is the kind of hand which recommends itself as an excellent three club bid for a non-vulnerable player. If you play the hand in three clubs doubled, you are assured of a good result, for the more you lose, the more you save.

There is always a possibility that your bid will prevent the opponents from reaching their best contract, and your hand is so useless for anything which your partner might want to bid, that you can hardly be interfering with the chances of your own side. This last factor is one of great importance ; a hand of this character :—

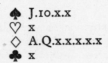

♠ J.10.x.x
♡ x
♦ A.Q.x.x.x.x.x
♣ x

should not be opened first or second hand with a bid of three diamonds because of the possibility that partner has a good hand, including a spade suit ; if this is the case, you will have prevented your own side from bidding game.

As a general proposition, a three bid should be avoided on any hand which contains two honour tricks, or four cards in a major suit (other than the suit bid), as such a hand cannot be regarded as hopeless.

RESPONDING TO THREE BIDS

Inexperienced players have great difficulty in making the correct response to an opening three bid of the type favoured by Acol players. The first point to realise is that the hand is decidedly weak, so that a very strong hand is required to make a game.

♠ K.Q.x.x.x
♡ x.x
♦ A.Q.x
♣ K.x.x

Over a three heart bid you might be tempted to call three spades or three no-trumps ; either call is hopeless. Pass and hope that three hearts is just made. It has become an accepted convention that if a player wishes to play in a game call in a suit other than that mentioned by his partner, he must call the game directly.

♠ A.K.Q.J.10.x
♡ K.x
◇ A.x.x
♣ Q.x

If partner bids three clubs, say four spades. A bid of
three spades would have an entirely different meaning. It
would be a control showing bid, and a slam invitation in
clubs.

♠ A.K.x.x
♡ K.x.x.x
◇ A.x
♣ A.x.x

Bid three spades over three diamonds or three clubs;
partner should recognise this as a slam invitation, and if
his three bid is a strong one, as three bids go, he can bid
five of his suit; if not, he will bid four only, and if your
side is vulnerable you can make another try with a four
no-trump bid; if partner still signs off, you should pass.

DEFENCE TO PRE-EMPTIVE BIDS

Most players use weak three bids nowadays and Acol
tactics are devised to deal with pre-emptive bids such
as the system uses itself. The normal tactics are to double
on good hands, and to bid three no-trumps on very strong
ones. The three no-trump bid requests partner to bid his
best suit, and to jump the bid if he is fairly strong.

♠ A.Q.10.x
♡ K.x.x
◇ K.x.x.x
♣ A.x

If first hand opens with a bid of three, and you hold this hand over him, you should double ; if partner happens to be very weak, you may get a bad result, as the double may be passed and the contract made ; but the risk of passing is greater than the risk of bidding.

♠ A.Q.x.x.
♥ A.J.x.x
♦ K.Q.x.x
♣ x

Double a bid of three spades, hearts or diamonds, hoping that partner will pass ; it is true that he may bid four clubs, but that risk must be taken. The tendency of recent years is to treat a double of a three call as primarily for penalties.

With a very strong hand and complete two-suiter make an overcall in the suit bid rather than say three no-trumps.

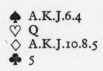

♠ A.K.J.6.4
♥ Q
♦ A.K.J.10.8.5
♣ 5

It would be very trying to have an opponent open three clubs in front of you here, but if it should happen, the bid is four clubs. The disadvantage of three no-trumps is that partner may fly high in hearts, placing you, as he is entitled to do, with an exceptionally fine all round hand and support for anything he may bid. It is true that when you bid four clubs, partner's most likely action is to bid four hearts : you then say four spades, and since you have ignored the suit in which he has responded partner should read you for a spade-diamond two-suiter and bid accordingly.

With a very strong one-suited hand, jump to game in the suit, or with fine all-round strength bid three no-trumps and then the suit.

It is true that there is no perfect way of dealing with opening three bids, and all methods have their defects; however, the best use must be found for the two overcalls available, double and three no-trumps, and that is the use which is recommended.

OPENING BIDS HIGHER THAN THREE

Opening bids of four in a major, and of four and five in a minor, are pre-emptive, and are made on hands which are too strong for three bids.

♠ x
♡ A.J.10.x.x.x.x.x
◇ K.x
♣ x.x

Systems in which the three bid is fairly strong might recommend three hearts, but the hand is too good for an Acol three bid, and the right call is four hearts.

CHAPTER X

SLAM BIDDING

*T*HE *Acol System makes use of all the usual devices for slam bidding, employing both cue bids and the four-five no-trump convention. But when all is said, the factor which above all leads to successful slam bidding, is intelligent bidding in the lower stages of the auction ; so long as each player bids his cards according to their worth, the road to slams is straight and sure.*

The natural character of Acol bidding provides an excellent foundation for slam bidding. Acol players bid the cards in front of them ; for tactical reasons a bid may be made which does not show the character of the hand, but false information is always remedied and partner is not left in the dark as to the distribution of strength.

A simple example will illustrate the difference between intelligent and purposeless bidding. You hold the following hand :—

♠ 10.x
♡ K.J.x
♢ K.x.x.x
♣ A.Q.x.x

Partner opens one spade, and you make your natural response of two no-trumps ; partner now says three diamonds ; what would you bid ? Nine players out of ten would say three no-trumps without thought ; the bid looks bad on paper, and bad it is, provided that partner is a good bidder, who can be relied upon not to make a stupid call.

An Acol player would have no hesitation in making the bid which on his cards is proper and natural — Four diamonds. He has already told his partner that his hand represents a two no-trump response, and partner should be able to judge from this whether the final contract should be three no-trumps or not ; if, with the information which he has received, partner calls another suit, it is only common sense that preference should be given ; partner may have hopes of a diamond slam, and a three no-trump reply is sure to stifle the bidding.

Needless to say, if partner's hand is :—

♠ A.K.10.x
♡ x.x
◇ A.Q.10.x
♣ J.x.x

he has made an atrocious call in bidding three diamonds, instead of three no-trumps.

The first principle of Acol slam bidding is to bid your cards naturally, to show your distribution as faithfully as you can, to avoid that class of " prepared " bid which presents a false picture of your hand — only on very rare occasions should a shorter suit be bid before a longer one ; to give preference, when your partner seems to want it, and to avoid unintelligent bids, such as three no-trumps by the responding hand in the above example, which arise from the common error of pre-judging the final contract.

INVITING A SLAM

The Acol System makes full use both of cue bids and of the four-five no-trump convention. Any system which confines itself to one or other of these methods, handicaps itself unnecessarily.

The choice between bidding four no-trumps and making a cue bid is often a delicate affair, and an example will best illustrate the considerations which should affect the decision. We will assume that the bidding has been :—

South	North
1 ♡	3 ♣
3 ◇	3 N-T
4 ♣	

The last bid is obviously a slam invitation, and what we have to consider is what would be the significance of the various bids open to North. He may give delayed support to one of his partner's bids ; otherwise he will bid five clubs, cue bid in spades, or say four no-trumps.

These bids are in ascending order of strength ; some example hands will show which bid should be preferred.

♠ K.Q.J
♡ Q.x
◇ x.x
♣ A.K.J.10.x.x

This is the least promising type of hand which North could hold. Acol players do not force lightly, and this is a borderline hand ; its playing strength just makes it worth a force, but once this has been done the player must sign off. His bid at the present stage should be the weakest available — five clubs ; when a game bid is inevitable, the minimum bid which a player can make is a bid of game.

♠ A.Q.J
♡ x.x
◇ J.x
♣ A.K.J.10.x.x

This is a better hand for purposes of slams, but North has already forced on it, and he should not become too excited. Although the technical requirements are held for a call of four no-trumps, that is not the right bid. North should compromise and cue bid his spade ace. The bid of four spades would say, " Now that you can support clubs, I am interested in the possibility of a slam ; I am not strong enough to invite a slam myself by bidding four no-trumps, but I am prepared to show my spade ace ; if you like to bid four no-trumps, well and good."

♠ A.Q.x
♡ K.x
♢ J.x
♣ A.K.J.10.x.x

The addition of the heart king makes a substantial difference. North is now confident of a slam, and can make the strongest bid open to him, four no-trumps, which tells South that he was only waiting for a further chance to invite a slam, and can guarantee six clubs, if South has two aces ; if not, he is prepared for South to bid whatever ace he holds, or alternatively to bid six clubs direct.

FOUR NO-TRUMPS BY THE WEAKER HAND

The above discussion must not lead to the impression that a four no-trump bid is always a sign of great encouragement. On occasions the bid may be almost a reluctant admission. This is the case where partner is, as it were, the leader of the bidding, and very clearly asks for a four no-trump bid, if the requirements for it are present. A fine example of this rare situation is the following :—

South	North
1 ♠	2 ♢
2 ♡	3 ♣
3 N-T	4 ♣

South's hand was :—

     ♠ A.Q.x.x
     ♡ K.10.x.x
     ◇ J.x
     ♣ A.x.x

This is such a moderate collection that South had to bid two hearts over two diamonds, because his hand was not strong enough for two no-trumps. Although South has not bid strongly, North has invited a slam, by taking the contract beyond the level of three no-trumps ; South should, therefore, make the response for which he has been clearly asked — four no-trumps. No great stress need be attached to the fact that North did not force ; having two minor suits to bid, he would refrain from forcing for considerations of time, even though the strength of his hand warranted a three diamond response. He probably holds something like :—

     ♠ x
     ♡ A.x
     ◇ A.Q.10.x.x
     ♣ K.J.10.x.x

On this type of hand North cannot bid the slam, unless he gets a four no-trump bid from his partner.

NEGATIVE USE OF FOUR-FIVE NO-TRUMP CONVENTION

The following hand from one of Waddington's Par Contests is a splendid example of the negative use to which the four-five no-trump convention can be put.

♠ K.9
♡ A.K.Q.3.2
♢ 5
♣ A.Q.9.5.3
      N

      S
♠ A.J.10.8
♡ 6.4
♢ A.K
♣ J.10.8.7.4

The recommended bidding is as follows :—

South		North
1 ♣		2 ♡
2 ♠		3 ♣
3 N-T		4 ♣
4 ♢		6 ♣
No bid		

North's bidding is very carefully thought out. Instead of bidding four no-trumps himself he so manoeuvres the auction that over four clubs South is very clearly invited to make the bid if he has the requirements for it. When he bids four diamonds, showing a good hand but denying the values of four no-trumps, North knows that one of the key cards, either an ace or the trump king, is missing, so he simply bids six clubs.

WHEN FOUR NO-TRUMPS IS NOT CONVENTIONAL

While the four no-trump convention is under discussion, a word must be said of the occasions when Acol players do not regard the bid as conventional. In general, the bid is

natural when partner's no-trump call is raised quantitatively ;
that is to say, when partner makes a bid of no trumps,
because he wants to play in no-trumps and not because he
is merely responding negatively, a raise of that no-trump
bid is natural.   The simplest example is :—

South	North
1 ♠	2 N-T
4 N-T	

It would be unintelligent to take South's bid as conventional ; if he wanted to know about his partner's aces,
it could only be because he held himself a very unbalanced
hand, and he would show this by bidding another suit.
The four no-trump bid says : " I have a balanced hand,
and a count of 20 to 21 ; if your two no-trump bid was
better than a minimum, we can play in six no-trumps."

Another situation, where the bid has a natural meaning,
is this :—

South	North
1 ♠	2 ♡
3 N-T	4 N-T

North is here raising a no-trump call which was made,
not by way of a negative response, as would have been the
case had North's bid been three hearts, but in order to
show a balanced hand containing about 18 to 21 points ;
North's four no-trump bid invites South to bid on, if his
hand is more than a minimum for his bid.   North holds
something of this kind :—

♠ Q.x
♡ A.Q.x.x.x
◇ K.10.x
♣ Q.x.x

If the four no-trumps is not regarded as natural in this situation, North is confronted with an impossible problem.

EXAMPLES OF SLAM BIDDING

Asking bids, according to the Culbertson definition, have no place in the Acol System, as they would continually obstruct the natural process of Acol bidding; it is felt, moreover, that whenever information of a special kind is required, the question can usually be conveyed by intelligent bidding. The hand which follows is of the type which is commonly adduced as a triumph for the two-way three bid, asking bids, and what-not; but in a fourteen-table duplicate pairs contest it was only the Acol players who reached the slam.

♠ A.K.Q.J.10.5
♡ 7
◇ A.8.6.4
♣ A.3
N

S

♠ 9.8.4
♡ A.J.9.5
◇ Q.9
♣ K.6.4.2

North was the dealer, and if playing the Culbertson System must open one spade or three spades; whichever bid he chooses, he is sure to be in difficulties on the next round. North has a perfect Acol two spade bid, to which South will respond three hearts; North repeats his spades, and South, although he has a useful hand, cannot at this stage bid more than four spades. North is clearly worth another try; his partner is known to have a fair hand, as he did not respond two no-trumps, nor did he give a simple raise to three spades. The most informative bid which North can make is five diamonds. The omission to bid four no-trumps need not disturb South on this occasion ; it is certain that North has the requirements for that bid, and the fact that he does not use it simply shows that he is interested in South's diamond holding.

The knowledge that North is concerned with diamonds is pleasing to South, who could bid six spades right away ; however, there is a possibility of a grand slam, if North has control of clubs ; that North has not got A.K of spades, A.K of diamonds and ace of clubs is certain from the fact that he did not start with a bid of two clubs ; but North might hold something like this :—

♠ A.K.Q.x.x.x.x
♡ K.x
♢ A.K.x.x
♣ None

South, therefore, bids five hearts over five diamonds ; if North follows with six clubs, South intends to bid six diamonds, showing the queen of that suit. As it is North bids five spades ; he has shown his hand, and still awaits South's verdict on the diamond situation ; South bids six spades ; his partner is known to hold eight playing tricks in spades for his Acol Two Bid, and he has shown further strength by his five diamond bid ; South is, therefore, confident that his hand will make up the gap to 12 tricks.

Another example of the exchange of information by means of cue bids and the four-five no-trump is the following hand :—

♠ K.10.2
♡ Q.7.3
◇ K.5.3.2
♣ A.7.6

N

S

♠ A.Q.9.8.7.3
♡ A.K.5.2
◇ A.4
♣ 5

The Acol bidding is as follows :—

South	North
1 ♠	2 N-T
3 ♡	4 ♠
4 N-T	5 ♣
5 N-T	6 ◇
6 ♡	7 ♠

The auction contains many points of interest. In the first place South almost has an Acol Two bid ; if he had the spade jack instead of a small one, he would say two spades. North's four spade bid over three hearts is clearly marked ; he has a sound two no-trump bid and support for both his partner's suits ; if he said only three spades, South might pass with a weak two-suiter. The next interesting call is South's five no-trumps. Since the response to four no-trumps was a positive one, the five no-trump bid shows three aces, at least one bid king, and willingness for a grand slam contract. North can almost respond with a direct seven spade bid ; his partner knows that he is missing one of the major suit kings (for with both and the club ace he would have responded five no-trump to four no-trump), and yet South is inviting a seven call ; however, North remembers that his partner has not started with a

D

two spade bid, so he temporises with six diamonds, a bid
which can only mean the king of that suit.   South's six
heart bid clearly indicates that his only concern by now is
third round control of hearts ;   North accordingly has no
hesitation in bidding the grand slam.

Seven spades is a lay-down if the trumps break 2—2 ;
if they are 3—1, declarer must play only two rounds
before testing the heart situation ;   if the hand with three
trumps also holds four hearts, the contract can still be made
through the use of this safety play. In certain circumstances
squeeze play would offer a slightly better chance.

OPENING BID OF FOUR NO-TRUMPS

On the principle that no bid should be wasted, the Acol
System has a special use for an opening bid of four no-
trumps ;   obviously this bid is not required to show a hand
of vast all-round strength, as that would be introduced
with a two club bid.

The four no-trump bid is reserved for those occasional
hands on which a player is interested solely in aces. The
response to the bid is five no-trumps with two aces, five
clubs with no aces, five spades, hearts or diamonds, with
the ace of that suit, and six clubs with the ace of clubs.
The " locus classicus " for this bid is hand 16 of the 1937
England v. Wales match.

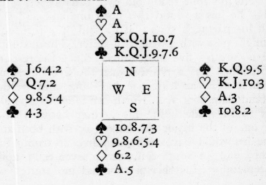

The North hand is perfectly suited to the Acol four no-trump opening; if partner responds five clubs, showing no aces, the hand is played in that contract; if he shows one ace, the contract is six clubs, and if two aces, seven clubs.

In the match, both pairs reached six clubs, but with exceptional difficulty. Lederer and Rose held the cards for England, and Lederer opened two clubs, a conventional bid on his system; Rose bid two diamonds, Lederer three clubs, Rose three hearts, Lederer four diamonds, and Rose five clubs; Lederer now went into one of his rare trances, and finally decided that Rose's preference probably showed the ace of clubs; he therefore bid six clubs, but when doubled was not sure enough of his deductions to redouble. The Acol bidding would have been four no-trumps, six clubs, no bid; and if doubled, North could redouble with confidence.

IMMEDIATE FOUR NO-TRUMPS RESPONSE

An immediate bid of four no-trumps, in response to an opening bid of one, does not show a giant all-round hand, but has its usual conventional significance. Partner has a five no-trump reply, if he holds the ace and king of the suit bid, as this represents the ordinary qualification of one ace and the kings of all the suits bid by the partnership. The immediate four no-trump bid is therefore used when interest centres only on the ace and king of the suit opened.

When this is all the responder wants to know, he should bid four no-trumps at once, as if he bids any other suits, the issue may never be settled for certain.

Example hand as follows :—

♠ A
♡ A.K.J.8.5.4
♢ Q.J.9.7
♣ A.8

This hand is from one of Waddington's Par Contests. Partner opened one diamond and the recommended response was four no-trumps, to determine beyond doubt whether partner had A.K of diamonds.

THE BLACKWOOD CONVENTION

The Blackwood convention, for showing aces and kings, had not been invented when Acol was first developed. The widespread popularity of the convention has not extended to Acol. In fact, it may be said that it is impossible to play " Acol and Blackwood." One can only play " Acol, *but* Blackwood."

CHAPTER XI

DEFENSIVE BIDDING

THE Acol System has no special conventions for defensive bidding, but at the same time its principles and standards are clearly defined.

We will consider in turn the use of the take-out double, simple and jump overcalls, and game-forcing overcalls.

USE OF TAKE-OUT DOUBLE

Acol players do not demand a very high standard of strength for take-out doubles, preferring a light double to a weak suit overcall.

♠ A.Q.6.2
♡ K.J.7
♢ A.8.5.3
♣ 7.6

If the player on your right opens one club you have to choose between passing, doubling, and bidding one spade ; the last bid is the worst, for if it is doubled you may have to play in one of the red suits at the range of two.

Provided that partner does not expect too much from a double, that is a better course than to pass, for if you do not speak now, you will never be able to, and the enemy may obtain the contract in two clubs when you could have made a part score or even a game in one of the majors.

THE TAKE-OUT INTO TWO CLUBS

When responding to a double partner should take out into two clubs on absolute weakness rather than bid another four-card suit at the range of two.

♠ Q.6.5.3
♡ 6.5.4.2
◇ 8.5
♣ 7.6.2

To a double of one diamond respond one spade, but if
one spade is doubled, two clubs should be preferred to
two hearts or one no-trump. As in the Culbertson System,
one no-trump in response to a double always shows a little
strength and does not guarantee a guard in the suit bid by
the opponents.

A RESPONSE IN THE SUIT DOUBLED

On a very strong hand, or on one which is certainly
worth a game in response to a double but offers a choice
of contract, respond with a bid in the suit doubled.

♠ K.Q.6.4
♡ A.10.8.5
◇ 8.3
♣ A.J.4

The proper response to a double of one diamond is
two diamonds : this is forcing to game.

BIDDING OVER A REDOUBLE

When third hand redoubles, the meaning of a pass by
fourth hand, the doubler's partner, is always a debated
point. A pass used to be regarded as a sign of strength,
showing that the player had defence to the bid of one
redoubled. Up to the present edition of this book that
was the correct Acol interpretation.

Most leading Acol players have now come round to the
other view. The penalty pass is so seldom useful that it

seems best to say that fourth player should pass if his hand is weak and has no feature worth showing. Culbertson players made this change some years ago, and it should now be regarded as part of the Acol System. If fourth hand *does* bid over the redouble, it is not to be assumed that he is strong, unless he makes a jump bid ; but if he passes, then his hand may be very weak.

SIMPLE OVERCALL

In the use of suit overcalls, Acol players use ordinary caution, taking care that the measure of risk is the measure of possible gain. A suit overcall is always preferred to a double on two-suited hands.

♠ A.8.7.5.3
♡ K.Q.10.7.5
♢ 4
♣ K.6

Over one diamond say one spade ; if you double there is a fear lest the partner of the opening bidder will jump high in diamonds, and you will never be able to show your two suits ; another possibility is that a double of one diamond will be left in, and that is sure to produce a bad result.

JUMP OVERCALL

A jump overcall is a strong bid and is preferred to a double on one-suited hands.

♠ A.Q.J.10.7.6
♡ K.5
♢ A.8.3
♣ Q.2

This hand is so strong that some players would double
an opening bid of, say, one heart ; it is better to bid two
spades, however, for if one heart is carried to four hearts
you will not know whether to double or bid four spades ;
but if you show your good suit at once, partner should be
able to judge what action to take.

The jump overcall is not forcing, but partner is expected
to respond on such values as he would require to reply
to an opening bid of one.

On very strong hands it is better to double and then
make a jump bid in your suit ; partner should raise on
about one playing trick.

GAME-FORCING OVERCALLS

The overcall by a defender in a suit bid by the opponents
is a force to game as in most systems.

An overcall by a defender of a one no-trump opening
with two no-trumps, shows a freak hand and is forcing
to game.

    ♠ K.Q.x.x.x.x
    ♡ None
    ♢ A.K.J.x.x.x
    ♣ A

A player holding this hand who bid four spades over an
opponent's no-trump bid was so unfortunate as to lose a
diamond ruff and three trump tricks, while six diamonds
was a lay-down. The hand is ideal for the no-trump
overcall : the bid is forcing to game, and partner should
take out into his best suit, with preference for the lower
valued when he has two of roughly equal strength, so that
the bidding of the presumed two-suiter may be facilitated.

CHAPTER XII

BRIEF SUMMARY

THE summary which follows is not intended to cover every branch of the system, but only such aspects of it as can be expressed in a condensed form.

There are certain situations in which it is possible to say that a certain bid indicates a certain amount of high card values. In summarising these high card values, the point count method is much more accurate than an honour trick table. It must be understood, however, that the point count requirements are in all cases approximate ; they assume balanced hands. In determining the correct bid the general make-up of the hand must always be taken into consideration, its suit lengths and intermediate values. So long as this reservation is kept in mind, the point count method serves as a useful guide for the treatment of balanced hands.

The point count : Ace=4, K=3, Queen=2, Jack=1. To have a play of three no-trumps on balanced hand you require 24-25 points. For small slam at no-trumps you require 34 points.

NO-TRUMP BIDDING

(a) Not Vulnerable

Opening one no-trump shows	.. ..	13 to 15 points
Raise to two no-trumps shows	.. ..	10 to 11 points
Raise to three no-trumps shows	.. ..	12 points
After a raise to two no-trumps the opener should bid three no-trumps on	.. ..	14 points

(b) Vulnerable

Opening one no-trump shows	.. ..	16 to 18 points
Raise to two no-trumps shows	.. ..	7 to 8 points
Raise to three no-trumps shows	.. ..	9 points
After a raise to two no-trumps the opener should bid three no-trumps on	.. ..	17 points

(c) Whether Vulnerable or Not

Opening two no-trumps shows	.. ..	20 to 22 points
Raise to three no-trumps shows	.. ..	5 points (sometimes 4)
Two clubs, followed by two no-trumps	..	23 points
Raise to three no-trumps shows	.. ..	3 points

A 22-point hand is on the borderline between a two no-trump and a two club bid.

Two clubs, followed by three no-trumps, shows 26 points.

An opening bid of three no-trumps may be a tactical call ; as a rule it shows a hand containing a long and strong minor suit, with protection in two other suits.

NO-TRUMP RESPONSES

It is assumed that partner has opened the bidding with a bid of one in a suit.

One no-trump shows	.. .. ..	5 to 9 points
Two no-trumps shows	.. .. ..	11 to 13 points
Three no-trumps shows	.. .. ..	14 to 16 points
(13 if the player has passed)		

NO-TRUMP REBIDS

(a) When partner has responded to your opening bid with a bid of one in a different suit :—

Two no-trumps shows	..	..	.. 17 to 18 points
Three no-trumps shows	..	..	.. 19 points

(*b*) When partner has responded to your opening bid with a bid of one no-trump :—

Two no-trumps shows	..	..	.. 17 to 18 points
Three no-trumps shows	..	..	.. 19 points

(*c*) When partner has responded to your opening bid with a simple take-out into two of a suit :—

Two no-trumps shows	..	..	.. 15 to 17 points
Three no-trumps shows	..	..	.. 18 points

Note.—The rebid requirements detailed in this section are calculated on a fairly conservative basis, and assume balanced hands ; where useful suit lengths and intermediate cards exist, the requirements can be shaded.

FORCING TO GAME

Forcing situations are less frequent in the Acol system than in orthodox Approach Forcing ; the following are the only bids which are unconditionally forcing to game :—

A two club bid, followed by any rebid other than two no-trumps.

South	West	North	East
2 ♣	No bid	2 ♦	No bid
2 ♡			

A jump take-out in a new suit, or a jump rebid in a new suit after partner has responded.

1 ♠	No bid	3 ♦	No bid
		or	
1 ♠	No bid	1 N-T	No bid
3 ♡			

An overcall in the opponents' suit, whether by the side which has opened the bidding or by the defenders, and an overcall of two no-trumps over an opening one no-trump.

1 ♡	No bid	1 ♠	2 ♣
3 ♣			

or

1 ♡	2 ♡		

or

1 N-T	2 N-T		

FORCING FOR ONE ROUND

A simple take-out into a new suit, provided that the responder has not previously passed.

South	West	North	East
1 ♡	No bid	1 ♠	

or

South	West	North	East
1 ♡	No bid	2 ◇	No bid

An Acol two bid.

2 ♠

FORCING BY INFERENCE

Certain bidding situations are easily recognisable as inferential forces ; the following are the commonest types of inferential force :—

A bid in a new suit, when partner has raised the first suit.

South	West	North	East
1 ♡	No bid	2 ♡	No bid
3 ♣			

A bid in a new suit, or a return to partner's major suit, when partner's opening bid or rebid is two no-trumps.

But a rebid of one's own suit over two no-trumps is generally a sign-off; see below, under Weakness Bids.

| 1 ♡ | No bid | 2 N-T | No bid |
| 3 ♣ | | | |

or

| 1 ♡ | No bid | 1 ♠ | No bid |
| 2 N-T | No bid | 3 ♡ | |

or

| 2 N-T | No bid | 3 ♡ | |

A bid in a new suit at the range of three, unless a sign-off bid has preceded.

| 1 ♡ | No bid | 2 ◇ | No bid |
| 3 ♣ | | | |

or

| 1 ♠ | No bid | 2 ◇ | No bid |
| 2 ♡ | No bid | 3 ♣ | |

Any bid which follows a jump rebid by partner; the only sign off is a pass.

| 1 ♡ | No bid | 2 ♣ | No bid |
| 3 ♡ | No bid | 4 ♣ | |

WEAKNESS BIDS

The following bids deny further strength beyond that already shown, and invite partner to pass; some of these bids, which are sign-off bids in the Acol System, are forcing in the Culbertson System.

Any simple take-out of an opening one no-trump bid.

| South | West | North | East |
| 1 N-T | No bid | 2 ♡ | |

A minimum rebid of one's own suit over partner's two no-trump bid.

1 ♡	No bid	2 N-T	No bid
3 ♡			

or

1 ♡	No bid	1 ♠	No bid
2 N-T	No bid	3 ♠	

or

1 ♠	No bid	2 ♡	No bid
2 N-T	No bid	3 ♡	

As in all systems, a series of minimum rebids in the same suit, whether by the opening bidder or by the responder, constitutes a determined sign-off.

1 ♣	No bid	1 ♡	No bid
2 ♣	No bid	2 ♢	No bid
3 ♣			

or

1 ♡	No bid	1 ♠	No bid
2 ♢	No bid	2 ♠	No bid
3 ♢	No bid	3 ♠	—

A return to partner's suit at the lowest level indicates a minimum raise.

1 ♠	No bid	2 ♠	No bid
3 ♡	No bid	3 ♠	

RESPONSES TO ACOL TWO BID

A response of two no-trumps shows less than two honour tricks.

A response of three no-trumps shows 10 to 12 points.

A bid of a new suit shows a biddable suit and not less than one honour trick.

A single raise shows adequate trump support (three small cards or as good as Q.x) and not less than one honour trick.

A double raise shows good distributional support, some high cards, but no aces.

ACOL TWO CLUB BID

The two club opening guarantees a minimum of five quick tricks.

For a positive response one of the following honour combinations is required :—

> An ace and a king.
>
> Four kings.
>
> Two king-queens.
>
> A king-queen and two kings.

A jump rebid by a player who has opened two clubs shows a solid trump suit and requests partner to bid any ace which he holds. Any further bid in a new suit demands that a king be shown.

CHAPTER XIII

SOME MISTAKES TO AVOID

NOT mistakes, exactly. Misguided practices, due to muddled thinking. This chapter shows some of the commonest ways in which points are lost, not through lack of system knowledge, but through want of judgment.

OVERBIDDING AFTER A PASS

It is extraordinary how many players, even in first class bridge, overcall their hands just because they have passed originally. You hold either of these hands :—

♠ 10.7.5.4.2   ♠ K.7.6.3
♡ 4   ♡ A.5.2
◇ A.4.3   ◇ 6 4
♣ K.10.7.6   ♣ A.9.7.3

You pass as first or second hand, your partner opens one spade and the next hand says no bid. Now what do you say? Thousands of players would make the overbid of four spades, instead of three spades, *because they had passed originally*.

It is the same with responses in no-trumps.

♠ K.J.7
♡ 7.6.4
◇ A.10.7.6
♣ K.J.9

Partner opens one heart, after you have passed. You have an obvious response of two no-trumps. Why overbid and say three no-trumps?

It is hardly an exaggeration to say that a hand on which it was right to pass originally can never be worth three no-trumps over an opening bid of one of a suit. Yet this sequence of bidding is extremely common.

A truism to which there is no answer is this :—

The fact that a player has passed does not make his hand any stronger.

FORCING AFTER A PASS

Just as players who have passed will overbid when raising partner's call, so do they often force without any justification.

♠ A.4
♡ A.10.7.6.3
♢ 7.5.2
♣ K.7.3

If partner has opened one diamond after three passes, then the prospects of game are naturally quite good. But there is not the slightest excuse for doing what many players would — making a jump bid of two hearts " to show that you had a good pass." Such bidding debases a forcing to game bid to a point at which it has no value.

A jump bid in a new suit after a pass means this :—If the opening bid is sound, then game is more or less a certainty. The meaning is the same as that of a force when the player has not passed, except of course that honour trick strength is limited by the original pass.

If the force after a pass is not regarded in this light, then a player who has passed on, say :—

♠ J.5
♡ A.Q.9.7.6.3
♢ Q.10.8.4.2
♣ None

has no way of bidding his hand when partner opens one
diamond. For this habit of jumping on moderate values
has become so common that the opening bidder no longer
takes the bid seriously and may stop short of game if his
hand is a minimum.

TAKING OUT A PENALTY DOUBLE

Now a different subject. You open one spade, the
opponent on your left overcalls with two hearts and partner
doubles. The next hand says no bid. You hold :—

♠ A.Q.10.7.5.2
♡ None
♢ K.10.4.3
♣ J.7.2

There are two schools of thought here. One says :—
" I daren't leave this in with a void in hearts and only
1½ to 2 defensive tricks. I must take out the double into
two spades."

The other argument is :—

" Obviously, as I am void of hearts, partner holds a
long string of them. Furthermore, he is probably short of
spades, so there is no point in rebidding this suit. It ought
to turn out a good double, so I will pass."

One of these analyses contains a profound fallacy.
Can you see what it is ?

The fallacy lies in the assumption that because you have
a void in hearts, partner necessarily has a great many.

All that you are entitled to conclude is that there are 13 hearts distributed among the other three hands. If the distribution is something like 5-4-4-0, or 6-4-3-0, partner's trumps may be of little use.

Another way to look at it is this :—a player with a void in the suit which has been doubled thinks this is an asset, because he places partner with a very strong holding ; then would this player be less pleased if he held one, two, or even three cards of the suit doubled ? Obviously not.

It is true that partner in the example above *may* have something like A.Q.J.10.x in hearts. But it is rather more likely that he has just a fair holding which will win disappointingly few tricks, sandwiched between the trumps of declarer and dummy. Partner's double should, therefore be protected ; you should take out the double into two spades.

OVERBIDS IN NO-TRUMPS

There is something about bids of no-trump which causes players, otherwise sound enough, to overcall. An example is the opening bid of one no-trump, not vulnerable. The accepted standard for this bid is 13 to 15 points. There is a modern school, however, which often opens one no-trump on 12, approves of 13, distrusts 14, and never makes the bid on 15.

No-one has ever advanced a good reason for so lowering the standard. The reason against it is this :—a balanced 12-point hand is always a good pass : if partner does not open, there is almost no chance of game. For a number of reasons it is not practicable to extend the limits of a no-trump bid beyond 3 points. Why, at the expense of a 15-point hand, include within these limits the 12-point hand which is better passed anyway ?

There are two other situations in which it has become fashionable to overcall. These are the responses of two and three no-trumps. The book says 11 to 13 for two no-trumps, 14 to 16 for three no-trumps. To-day many players respond two no-trumps on 10 to 12, three no-trumps on 13 and 14, reluctantly on 15.

The point which players miss when they stretch these responses is this :—Although two no-trumps is a limit bid, not forcing, nevertheless in principle it is not a bid in which one likes to finish. Therefore, in any sensible system a bid of two no-trumps should be avoided unless it is highly probable that game will be reached. That is the argument against reducing the response of two no-trumps to 10 to 12, instead of 11 to 13. If that is done, partner has to pass two no-trumps more often, and that is not desirable.

As for responding three no-trumps on 13 points, what is wrong about this is simply that there are a few hands which are fair opening bids but which will not make game with a barren 13 points opposite.

♠ A.J.9.4
♡ 8.3
◇ 7.5.2
♣ A.K.6.3

This is a reasonable opening bid, but if partner has exactly 13 points and no five card suit, game will be very hard work in three no-trumps. Beside balanced hands like this, there are the light Acol openings with a six card suit and $1\frac{1}{2}$ to 2 honour tricks. Here again the leeway afforded by a response of two no-trumps on 13 points is very welcome.

PREPARED BIDS AND REVERSES

Many Acol players have confused ideas about the significance in the system of reverse bids. This example was given on page 9 :—

♠ A.K.x.x
♡ K.10.x.x.x
◇ Q.x
♣ x.x

On such a moderate hand it is wise to open one spade, because a bidding sequence such as one heart — two clubs — two spades is unsound on these minimum values. That is easy to understand. Where some players go wrong is in assuming that when the hand is strong there is some advantage in reversing even if it means bidding suits in unnatural order. So with :—

♠ A.Q.x.x
♡ A.K.x.x
◇ K.Q.x
♣ x.x

the proper opening bid is one spade, in accordance with the general rule that when suits are of equal length the higher valued should be bid first. There is no sense whatsoever in opening one heart so that, by making a reverse bid of two spades on the next round, you can indicate that you have a strong hand.

It often happens, of course, that the lower valued of two four card suits has to be bid first. For example, on :—

♠ A.Q.7.2
♡ 8.4
◇ Q.8.3
♣ K.Q.9.4

the only possible opening is one club. If one spade is opened, there is no sound rebid over two hearts. But when the suits are adjacent, such as spades and hearts, there is no need for this type of prepared bid and to bid hearts and follow with spades must show longer hearts than spades.

CHAPTER XIV

TACTICAL AND COMPETITIVE BIDDING

COMPETITIVE bidding is something apart from systems, but nevertheless Acol players have a very definite "attitude of mind" towards competitive situations. As S. J. Simon points out in his introduction to this book, bidding is not a conversation between partners but a struggle between opposing sides. Recognising this, Acol players believe in getting their blow in first. They make light opening bids, light informatory doubles and, compared with the Baron System, for example, light over-calls. Once the bidding is under way, the more they can bounce the opponents, the better.

When there is a choice between an honest raise of partner's suit and a delicate approach bid, the Acol method is always to raise.

♠ 8
♡ 10.7.6.4
◇ A.J.7.5.2
♣ K.6.3

If partner opens one heart, it is much better to raise immediately to three hearts than to make the approach bid of two diamonds, whose only effect can be to make it easier for the opponents to come in with spades.

A little imagination and enterprise is worth much more than " exact " bidding in a position like this.

♠ 8.4
♡ K.J.10.7.5
◇ A.J.6.3
♣ J.2

Not vulnerable, you open one heart third hand after two passes. West passes, North says two hearts and East passes. Now of course, two hearts is the most you can expect to make. However, if you pass, it is extremely unlikely, especially against strong opponents, that you will buy the contract. Although West passed on the first round, it is fairly certain that he will reopen the bidding if you pass, either with a double or with two spades. If you bid three hearts, you will probably stop West bidding, but partner will probably give you four hearts and after this bidding the opponents may well double. If, on the other hand, you bid four hearts yourself, it is most unlikely that you will be doubled. East could not open the bidding and West had nothing to say on the first round over one heart ; so it is improbable that either can double four hearts bid in this way. To go two down undoubled, losing 100, is sure to be a fine result on the deal, probably a " top " in match point play.

The records of tournament play are full of hands in which an Acol team has played a hand·in both rooms, often scoring points at both tables. Players who are very cautious about their defensive overbids succeed in avoiding penalty doubles, but time and again they are outbid in both rooms.

PROTECTIVE BIDDING

Systems which insist on strong overcalls compensate for this by making it a rule that when the opponents stop bidding the partner of a player who has not passed originally should, whenever possible, reopen the bidding to protect partner's pass. If an opening bid is followed by two passes, some players will hardly ever pass ; they find a bid of some kind on such minimum values as a king and a couple of queens. This is quite unnecessary at Acol, because it is not part of the Acol style to make

trap passes on strong hands. If an opponent opens
one heart and you hold :—

♠ A.8
♡ K.Q.10.8
◇ K.J.3.2
♣ A.10.3

don't make a cunning pass, but double and see what
happens. Defensive bidding becomes hopelessly unbalanced if you say no bid and place on partner's shoulders
the responsibility of protecting your hand.

LIGHT OPENING BIDS

Some players allow their judgment to be upset when
competitive bidding follows a light opening bid. The
first rule is not to panic. If you have opened light and
partner doubles at a fairly high range, give partner credit
for realising that you may not have more than a couple
of honour tricks. Don't rescue unless partner has
supported your suit and you know that you can bid on
without heavy loss.

A useful lesson is contained in this example of bidding
tactics :—

♠ A.Q.10.8.6.3
♡ J
◇ K.10.9.5
♣ 10.4

As South you open one spade, West says two hearts,
North three spades, and East four hearts. Now it seems
obvious that you should bid four spades, partly because
you may well make it and partly because four hearts is
probably on for the opponents. So you bid four spades,

West says five hearts and partner doubles. Now you have a difficult decision. You are weak in high cards and cannot be sure of defeating five hearts. You have to guess whether or not to go five spades.

You can avoid this dilemma by passing on the previous round. When four hearts comes round to your partner, he will either double or go four spades. If partner doubles four hearts, you bid four spades and leave future action to partner, having warned him that a double does not suit you. If partner goes to four spades over four hearts, then if the opponents go five hearts, you go five spades, whether partner doubles or not.

DOUBLING AFTER A PASS

An informatory double by a player who has passed is an effective weapon which is often overlooked.

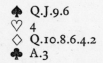

♠ Q.J.9.6
♡ 4
◇ Q.10.8.6.4.2
♣ A.3

After you have passed, the opponent on your left opens one heart and his partner bids two clubs. Now you may hazard two diamonds, of course, if you are not vulnerable, but the best bid, and not many players would think of it, is double. The advantage of doubling is that, if partner has a fair spade suit, you will be able to sacrifice cheaply in four spades.

DOUBLING THE BID IN SIGHT

When opponents are bidding round the clock, a defender often finds himself with one of the enemy suits held strongly but not much outside. When this happens, most players account it a virtue not to double, for fear of

pushing the opponents into a better contract. This form
of caution is very much overdone. If you follow the
principle of doubling what is under your nose, every
now and again you will push opponents out of something
they cannot make into something they can, but in the
long run you will pick up thousands and thousands of
points which cautious players smugly forego. Nine
times out of ten partner can double the feared switch.
A hand from the 1947 *Daily Telegraph* Cup final is a
striking instance of this phobia.

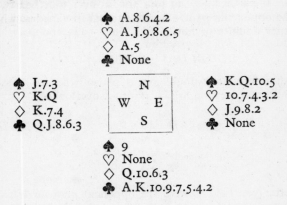

```
                        ♠ A.8.6.4.2
                        ♡ A.J.9.8.6.5
                        ◇ A.5
                        ♣ None

  ♠ J.7.3          ┌─────────┐      ♠ K.Q.10.5
  ♡ K.Q           │    N    │      ♡ 10.7.4.3.2
  ◇ K.7.4         │ W     E │      ◇ J.9.8.2
  ♣ Q.J.8.6.3     │    S    │      ♣ None
                  └─────────┘
                        ♠ 9
                        ♡ None
                        ◇ Q.10.6.3
                        ♣ A.K.10.9.7.5.4.2
```

The hand was played at 10 tables. North was dealer,
and reasonable bidding goes like this :—

South	West	North	East
		1 ♡	No bid
2 ♣	No bid	2 ♠	No bid
4 ♣	No bid	4 ◇	No bid
5 ♣			

At this point it is ludicrous, especially at match point
play, for West not to double. If five clubs is taken back
into five hearts it is most unlikely that this will be made.

Yet at most tables West passed when the bidding reached five clubs and at two tables the hand was played in *Six* clubs undoubled.

S. J. Simon was one of the West players and he, against some hesitant bidding which gave little picture of South's strength, nearly went too far by doubling four clubs. On the lead of a heart this can be made by good play. Declarer plays ace and another heart, ruffing in his hand, then lays down ace of clubs. At this point it is essential to play ace of spades and ruff a spade, the object being to reduce West's cards of exit. The ten of clubs follows and West exits with his third spade. Declarer ruffs and plays nine of clubs. This is the position :—

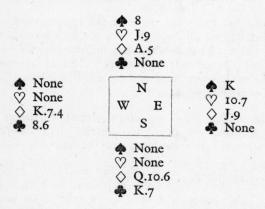

West is on play and must give up a trick in either diamonds or clubs. South makes four clubs, losing just three trump tricks or two trumps and a diamond.

CHAPTER XV

TWO CLUBS OVER ONE NO-TRUMP

THE chapter which deals with responses to no-trump openings has been left unaltered in this edition, but since the last edition a new bid of considerable importance has taken hold among a number of good Acol players. This is a conventional response of two clubs to an opening one no-trump bid.

The new bid takes the place of the conventional three club bid described on page 28. Its object is to deal with all those awkward hands which are difficult to gauge when partner has opened one no-trump. The convention is still in the exploratory stage and we will begin by outlining the bids suggested by Jack Marx.

The responder bids two clubs almost whenever the eventual contract is open to doubt. The no-trump opener then rebids in accordance with the following rules :—

(1) If he has four cards in either major, he bids two of that suit. If he holds four cards in both majors, he bids spades first and hearts later if he has the opportunity.

(2) With no four-card major and a minimum no-trump he rebids two diamonds.

(3) With no four card major, and a better than minimum no-trump he rebids two no-trumps.

Subsequent bidding is on commonsense lines, as the following examples will show :—

```
♠ A.8.4                    ♠ K.10.7.5.3
♡ K.5          W   E       ♡ A.8.4.2
♦ Q.10.8.3                 ♦ 6.3
♣ A.9.6.2                  ♣ K.5
```

West opens one no-trump not vulnerable and East responds two clubs. Having no four-card major and moderate no-trump West rebids two diamonds. East now bids two spades. This is not forcing, but it is more encouraging than a simple response of two spades to one no-trump would have been. That would be the right bid on East's hand if a small club were held instead of the king. Furthermore, there is a strong inference that the spades are a five card suit. So, although his no-trump is a minimum, West can raise to three spades, and so a rather close game is reached. Four spades is a better contract than three no-trumps.

```
♠ K.J.4                    ♠ 5
♡ A.J.2        W   E        ♡ K.7.6.3
♦ A.10.3                   ♦ Q.7.6.5.4.2
♣ K.J.10.5                 ♣ Q.9
```

West opens a vulnerable no-trump. Not vulnerable, East would bid simply two diamonds. Vulnerable, there is a chance of better things, so East responds two clubs. West has a 17 point hand with two 10's, so he rebids two no-trumps rather than two diamonds. East still cannot be sure of game, so he says three diamonds. This minor suit rebid is not forcing to game even though West rebid two no-trumps. It proclaims an unbalanced hand with a long minor suit which lacks the tops. West should pass, because his diamonds are not good enough for the gamble of three no-trumps. If West had had the king of diamonds instead of the king of clubs, he could have chanced three no-trumps.

Ordinary raises to two and three no-trumps show the
same values as at present.   Responder can force by
making an immediate jump in a suit or by responding
two clubs and making a jump bid if the opener says two
diamonds.   Marx suggests that an immediate jump take-
out should be strong, showing the sort of hand which is
worth a force in response to an opening suit bid.

That the convention represents an advance on present
methods is beyond doubt.   An indirect advantage of the
bid is that a player with a four card major suit can open
one no-trump more freely than at present, without the fear
that a better contract may be missed in the major. The only
disadvantage of the convention is that the weakness take-
out to two clubs is taken away.   Responder must simply
pass on a hand like this :—

$$\spadesuit \text{ x.x.x}$$
$$\heartsuit \text{ J.x.x.x}$$
$$\diamondsuit \text{ x}$$
$$\clubsuit \text{ K.x.x.x.x}$$

Note that it is not sound to bid two clubs, intending to
bid three clubs on the next round, for that shows a hand
which offers some play for game at no-trumps.

The convention is only in the exploratory stage.   Some
Acol experts dislike the two no-trump rebid on better
than minimum hands.   They regard the bid as obstructive,
and indeed in some cases it is.   If to bid two clubs, followed by
two hearts, is regarded as equivalent to bidding two and a half
hearts, then there seems to be no need for the two no-trump
rebid.   Some players, again, dispute that two clubs followed
by two hearts is in any way more encouraging than a direct
two hearts.   They reduce the convention to an understanding
that over two clubs the no-trump opener should bid a four
card major if he has one, and otherwise should say two diamonds.

Improvements can probably be made in the system of forcing responses. Hands like this are very difficult to bid over an opening vulnerable no-trump.

♠ Q.9.7.5.3.2
♡ 8
♢ A.J.6.4.3
♣ A

If partner has the right cards, a slam will be laid down, but if he has not, than a contract of five may fail. There is something to be said for a convention whereby a response of three spades is a slam invitation and a form of asking bid. With none of the three top honours in spades the opener should rebid three no-trumps. With one of the tops but no outside ace, he should also bid three no-trumps. With one of the tops and an outside ace, he should bid the lowest valued ace. And with two of the top honours he should raise to four spades ; then other controls can be located through a conventional four no-trump bid.

The bids suggested in the last paragraph have no place at all in the system at present ; but they show the lines along which the convention may develop.

THE
SYSTEM AT WORK

THE SYSTEM AT WORK

Illustrations from

International Matches of 1949

"IT may come as a shock to any followers, but I admit cheerfully that in theory some of these other systems are just as good as, if not better, than mine. But this in theory only. In practice I am still convinced that my system has a clear advantage over all the others, because it achieves its results with the minimum effort."

Thus, in 1936, wrote Richard Lederer of his own system. And now in 1949 its advocates are fully justified in making the same claim for the Acol system. Except that they can carry the claim even further; for not only does the system facilitate bidding for its exponents, it also does a great deal to destroy the communications of its opponents. The limit raise, a special feature of the system, time and again hamstrings the opponents by making them guess at too high a level.

But the principles of the system have been adequately dealt with in the preceding chapters. In the next few pages we propose to illustrate the system at work. The most famous Acol quartette, M. Harrison-Gray, K. Konstam, Terence Reese and B. Shapiro had a season of superlative success in 1949. Representing Crockford's Club they outplayed and convincingly beat the American champion team for the Crowninshield Cup.

In this match there was an interesting conflict of systems. On the one hand the Acol system of the British team and on the other an approach system reinforced with the "weak two" and with other novel theory. The American style seeks to make defence difficult — their heavy indulgence in the " waiting bid " of a three card suit results in their having made so many bids before arriving at their final spot that the opponent often misreads their hands and the location of specific values. But the sword is two-edged : often the direct thrust of the Acol limit raise, and particularly in defensive bidding, destroyed their communications and often again, where the Acol players were permitted to enter the bidding at a low level, their opponents were not granted the same indulgence.

There was a further contrast of style in the no-trump bidding — the strict Milton Work point count of the Acol system against a no-trump based on a combination of honour tricks and honour cards. Here again the Acol theory seemed to triumph.

None would dispute that this match was decided by the bidding supremacy of the winners. In the ninety-six board match the Acol team bid and made eight games, none of which were bid by the Americans. And there was no counterbalancing story of games bid and not made. The effect of this was an edge far too great for one good team to concede to another.

In the Appendix that follows a selection of hands has been made designed to illustrate these features. They are not calculated to create the impression that all the triumphs were with Acol and none with the American style, but rather to show the special features of the Acol system at work in the hands of experts and against experts.

The same four players and Adam Meredith were the Acol-playing spearhead of a British team which for the second year in succession won the Open European Championship, and here again we saw, in match after match, triumphs for the Acol principle that attack is the best defence. The Acol light opening bid and the Acol limit raise time and again enabled our players to buy the contract, often with cards on which their opponents were unable to even enter the bidding. The hands selected out of these championships are few out of many which would have illustrated the same points.

CROCKFORD'S *v.* U.S.A. (BOARD 10)

ROOM 1	ROOM 2
N. Reese	*N.* Rapee
S. Shapiro	*S.* Stayman
E. Leventritt	*E.* Konstam
W. Crawford	*W.* Gray

```
                    ♠ Q.9.5
                    ♡ 7.6.5.2
                    ◇ A.9.3
                    ♣ Q.4.2
    ♠ 10          ┌─────────┐      ♠ K.6.4.2
    ♡ A.J.8.3     │    N    │      ♡ Q.9
    ◇ J.10.7.6.2  │  W   E  │      ◇ 8.4
    ♣ A.7.5       │    S    │      ♣ K.J.10.8.3
                  └─────────┘
                    ♠ A.J.8.7.3
                    ♡ K.10.4
                    ◇ K.Q.5
                    ♣ 9.6
```

Dealer West.   Game All.

ROOM 1

West	North	East	South
No	No	No	1 ♠
Dble	No	1 N-T	No
2 ◇	No	No	No

Final Declaration : 2 ◇
Card led : Queen of spades
West obtained 7 tricks
N-S + 100

ROOM 2

West	North	East	South
No	No	No	1 ♠
Dble	2 ♣	3 ♣	No
No	No		

Final Declaration : 3 ♣
Card led : 9 of clubs
East obtained 9 tricks
E-W + 110

NET RESULT OF BOARD + 210 TO CROCKFORD'S

CROCKFORD'S *v.* U.S.A. (Board 10)

This hand is introduced to illustrate the light distributional double by a hand which has previously passed. Rapee's response of two spades forced Konstam into the superior contract of clubs, but he would probably have bid two clubs rather than one no-trump in any case, since West's double was obviously strongly distributional.

CROCKFORD'S *v.* U.S.A. (BOARD 11)

ROOM 1

    N. Reese
    S. Shapiro
    E. Leventritt
    W. Crawford

ROOM 2

    N. Rapee
    S. Stayman
    E. Konstam
    W. Gray

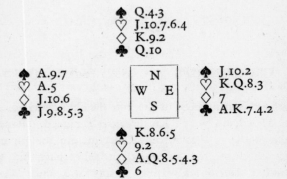

♠ Q.4.3
♡ J.10.7.6.4
◇ K.9.2
♣ Q.10

♠ A.9.7   ♠ J.10.2
♡ A.5   ♡ K.Q.8.3
◇ J.10.6   ◇ 7
♣ J.9.8.5.3   ♣ A.K.7.4.2

♠ K.8.6.5
♡ 9.2
◇ A.Q.8.5.4.3
♣ 6

Dealer : NORTH   Love All.

ROOM 1

North	East	South	West
No	1 ♣	1 ◇	1 ♠
2 ◇	2 ♠	3 ◇	3 ♡
No	4 ♣	No	No
No			

Final Declaration : 4 ♣
Card led : Ace of diamonds
East obtained 11 tricks
E-W + 150

ROOM 2

North	East	South	West
No	1 ♣	1 ◇	3 ♣
No	3 ♡	No	5 ♣
No	No	No	

Final Declaration : 5 ♣
Card led : Ace of diamonds
East obtained 11 tricks
E-W + 400

NET RESULT OF BOARD + 250 TO CROCKFORD'S

CROCKFORD'S *v.* U.S.A. (BOARD 11)

A beautiful Acol sequence by Gray and Konstam. Gray's bid of three clubs is the Acol limit bid, Konstam invites game with three hearts and Gray, with two aces and no diamond control, makes a splendid bid of five clubs.

Compare the American sequence of waiting bids " gone mad." West at no stage bids his excellent clubs and East suppresses his heart suit, even after his partner has bid them.

Note also that West's " approach " of one spade permits North to take a hand in the bidding.

CROCKFORD'S *v.* U.S.A. (BOARD 17)

ROOM 1	ROOM 2
N. Konstam.	*N.* Rapee
S. Gray	*S.* Stayman
E. Leventritt	*E.* Shapiro
W. Crawford	*W.* Reese

```
                    ♠ J.10.9.5.3
                    ♡ A.7.3
                    ◇ None
                    ♣ J.6.5.4.3

 ♠ A.Q.2            ┌─────────┐        ♠ K.7
 ♡ J.5.2            │    N    │        ♡ 10.9.4
 ◇ K.Q.J.7.4.2      │ W     E │        ◇ A.8.6.5
 ♣ 10               │    S    │        ♣ K.9.8.7
                    └─────────┘
                    ♠ 8.6.4
                    ♡ K.Q.8.6
                    ◇ 10.9.3
                    ♣ A.Q.2
```

Dealer : SOUTH   Game All.

ROOM 1					ROOM 2			
South	*West*	*North*	*East*		*South*	*West*	*North*	*East*
No	1 ◇	No	1 ♡		No	1 ◇	No	3 ◇
No	2 ◇	No	2 N-T		No	3 ♣	No	3 N-T
No	3 ♡	No	3 N-T		No	No	No	
No	No	No						

ROOM 1	ROOM 2
Final Declaration : 3 N-T	Final Declaration : 3 N-T
Card led : 8 of spades	Card led : King of hearts
East obtained 9 tricks	East obtained 8 tricks
E-W + 600	N-S + 100

NET RESULT OF BOARD + 700 TO U.S.A.

CROCKFORD'S *v.* U.S.A. (BOARD 17)

This illustrates a successful " waiting bid " of the type favoured, perhaps to excess, by the Americans. In this case it succeeded in inhibiting the fatal heart lead. Later, when our players were more familiar with their style, it might well have had the opposite effect of encouraging it.

CROCKFORD'S *v.* U.S.A. (BOARD 22)

ROOM 1   ROOM 2

   N. Konstam   *N.* Rapee
   S. Gray   *S.* Stayman
   E. Leventritt   *E.* Shapiro
   W. Crawford   *W.* Reese

                           ♠ J.10.9.7.5.4
                           ♡ 9.3
                           ♢ A.3
                           ♣ J.5.3

  ♠ Q   ♠ 3
  ♡ Q.8.2   N   ♡ K.J.7.6.5
  ♢ K.Q.J.9   W   E   ♢ 8.7.6.5.2
  ♣ A.K.Q.10.4   S   ♣ 6.2

                           ♠ A.K.8.6.2
                           ♡ A.10.4
                           ♢ 10.4
                           ♣ 9.8.7

Dealer : WEST   Game All.

        ROOM 1   ROOM 2

West	*North*	*East*	*South*	*West*	*North*	*East*	*South*
1 ♢	No	1 ♡	1 ♠	1 ♣	No	1 ♡	1 ♠
2 ♣	3 ♣	4 ♢	4 ♠	2 ♢	2 ♠	3 ♢	No
5 ♢	Double			3 ♡	No	4 ♡	No
				No	No		

Final Declaration : 5 ♢ doubled   Final Declaration : 4 ♡
Card led : Jack of spades   Card led : Ace of spades
West obtained 10 tricks   East obtained 10 tricks
N-S + 200   E-W + 620

     NET RESULT OF BOARD + 820 TO CROCKFORD'S

CROCKFORD'S *v.* U.S.A. (BOARD 22)

A triumph for the Acol theory of limit bids. When South is able to bid one spade, North, Konstam, knows that three spades must be a worthwhile contract and makes the bid, enabling Gray to make the fine sacrifice bid of four spades.

In the other room, once Rapee had bid two spades only, North-South were in difficulties. If North is subsequently able to bid three spades, South will still not bid four in view of North's first effort.

CROCKFORD'S *v.* U.S.A. (BOARD 60)

ROOM 1

- *N.* Konstam
- *S.* Gray
- *E.* Leventritt
- *W.* Crawford

ROOM 2

- *N.* Rapee
- *S.* Stayman
- *E.* Reese
- *W.* Shapiro

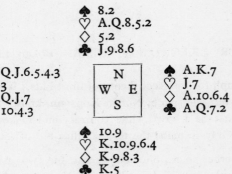

♠ 8.2
♥ A.Q.8.5.2
♦ 5.2
♣ J.9.8.6

♠ Q.J.6.5.4.3
♥ 3
♦ Q.J.7
♣ 10.4.3

♠ A.K.7
♥ J.7
♦ A.10.6.4
♣ A.Q.7.2

♠ 10.9
♥ K.10.9.6.4
♦ K.9.8.3
♣ K.5

Dealer : EAST

East and West Vulnerable.

ROOM 1			
East	*South*	*West*	*North*
1 N-T	No	2 ♠	No
No	No		

ROOM 2			
East	*South*	*West*	*North*
1 ♣	No	1 ♠	No
3 ♠	No	4 ♠	No
No	No		

Final Declaration : 2 ♠
Card led : 5 of diamonds
West obtained 10 tricks
E-W + 170

Final Declaration : 4 ♠
Card led : 5 of diamonds
West obtained 10 tricks
E-W + 620

NET RESULT OF BOARD + 450 TO CROCKFORD'S

CROCKFORD'S *v.* U.S.A. (BOARD 60)

At Acol an opening bid of one no-trump on the East hand would be unthinkable. Certainly, over one no-trump the weakness take-out of two spades is the only bid available to West.

The Reese-Shapiro sequence is routine Acol bidding. Over a response of one heart, Reese would have bid two no-trumps — over one spade, he bids the full value of his hand, and Shapiro, with his additional distributional values, has no hesitation in bidding the game.

CROCKFORD'S *v.* U.S.A. (BOARD 74)

ROOM 1

- *N.* Reese
- *S.* Shapiro
- *E.* Leventritt
- *W.* Crawford

ROOM 2

- *N.* Rapee
- *S.* Stayman
- *E.* Konstam
- *W.* Gray

```
            ♠ A.Q.5
            ♡ 10.8.6
            ◇ 10.7.3
            ♣ 6.5.4.3
  ♠ 9.6.2        N        ♠ K.10.3
  ♡ 7.4       W     E     ♡ K.Q.J.2
  ◇ J.9.8        S        ◇ K.Q.5.2
  ♣ A.Q.J.9.2             ♣ K.10
            ♠ J.8.7.4
            ♡ A.9.5.3
            ◇ A.6.4
            ♣ 8.7
```

Dealer : WEST   Game All.

ROOM 1					ROOM 2			
West	*North*	*East*	*South*		*West*	*North*	*East*	*South*
No	No	1 ♡	No		No	No	1 N-T	No
1 N-T	No	No			3 N-T	No	No	No

Final Declaration : 1 N-T

Card led : 6 of clubs

West obtained 10 tricks

E-W + 180

Final Declaration : 3 N-T

Card led : 4 of spades

East obtained 8 tricks

N-S + 100

NET RESULT OF BOARD + 280 TO U.S.A.

CROCKFORD'S *v.* U.S.A. (Board 74)

Although the Americans gained points on this board, three no-trumps was a very desirable contract since only a spade lead could defeat it, and the chance of a vulnerable game was too good to miss. For the Acol no-trump count, the bidding is routine. Using the Culbertson honour trick count, the hand does not qualify for a no-trump opening, and West, not unnaturally, is reluctant to respond at the two level.

It may be argued that East could have " chanced his arm " with a bid of two no-trumps. Had he done so, he would have been guessing — the Acol players *knew* that they had game-going values.

Note that the fifth club in West's hand is worth an extra point, hence Gray's correct response of three no-trumps.

CROCKFORD'S v. U.S.A. (BOARD 83)

ROOM 1	ROOM 2
N. Konstam	*N.* Rapee
S. Gray	*S.* Stayman
E. Leventritt	*E.* Shapiro
W. Crawford	*W.* Reese

```
                    ♠ A.2
                    ♡ J.9.7.3.2
                    ◇ K.9.8.4
                    ♣ 9.4
    ♠ J.9.4           ┌───────┐        ♠ 10.8.7.6
    ♡ 10              │   N   │        ♡ A.K.8
    ◇ A.Q.7         W │     E │        ◇ 5.3.2
    ♣ A.K.J.8.6.2     │   S   │        ♣ Q.7.3
                      └───────┘
                    ♠ K.Q.5.3
                    ♡ Q.6.5.4
                    ◇ J.10.6
                    ♣ 10.5
```

Dealer : NORTH   North and South Vulnerable.

ROOM 1

North	East	South	West
No	No	No	1 ♣
No	1 ♠	No	2 ♠
No	No	No	

ROOM 2

North	East	South	West
No	No	No	1 ♣
No	1 ♠	No	3 ♣
No	3 N-T	No	No
No			

Final Declaration : 2 ♠

Card led : Jack of diamonds

West obtained 8 tricks

E-W + 110

Final Declaration : 3 N-T

Card led : 4 of hearts

East obtained 9 tricks

E-W + 400

NET RESULT OF BOARD + 290 TO CROCKFORD'S

CROCKFORD'S *v.* U.S.A. (BOARD 83)

Another triumph for the directness of Acol as opposed to the over-elaboration of the American " approach." Three clubs is the natural bid. It does not cut out a spade contract, for East with five spades can rebid them, and if East makes a waiting bid in diamonds or hearts, West will have an opportunity to show delayed spade support.

CROCKFORD'S *v.* U.S.A. (BOARD 96)

ROOM 1	ROOM 2
N. Konstam	*N.* Rapee
S. Gray	*S.* Stayman
E. Leventritt	*E.* Shapiro
W. Crawford	*W.* Reese

        ♠ 10.8.2
        ♡ Q.7.5.2
        ◇ A.J.6.5.4
        ♣ 9

♠ A.Q.J   ♠ K.7.6.4
♡ K.J.8.3   N   ♡ 6.4
◇ 10   W   E   ◇ K.Q.9.2
♣ K.Q.10.5.4   S   ♣ J.3.2

        ♠ 9.5.3
        ♡ A.10.9
        ◇ 8.7.3
        ♣ A.8.7.6

Dealer : EAST   Game All

ROOM 1

East	South	West	North
No	No	1 ♣	No
1 ◇	No	1 ♡	No
1 ♠	No	2 ♣	No
No	No		

Final Declaration : 2 ♠
Card led : 3 of spades
East obtained 8 tricks
E-W + 110

ROOM 2

East	South	West	North
No	No	1 ♣	No
1 ◇	No	2 N-T	No
3 N-T	No	No	No

Final Declaration : 3 N-T
Card led : 5 of diamonds
West obtained 10 tricks
E-W + 630

NET RESULT OF BOARD + 520 TO CROCKFORD'S

CROCKFORD'S *v.* U.S.A. (BOARD 96)

Three no-trumps seems the obvious contract on these hands. Although Crawford regards his bid of two spades as quite strong in this situation (stronger than the same bid would be regarded at Acol) Leventritt found himself unable to produce another bid.

Reese's bid of two no-trumps might shock the purist, because of his singleton diamond. It is a well-judged commonsense bid, however, since the spade and heart tenaces make no-trumps, with West as declarer, an inviting prospect. And even if West bid one heart, the normal Acol sequence would be :

1 ♣	1 ♢
1 ♡	1 N-T
2 N-T	3 N-T

GT. BRITAIN *v.* IRELAND (BOARD 22)

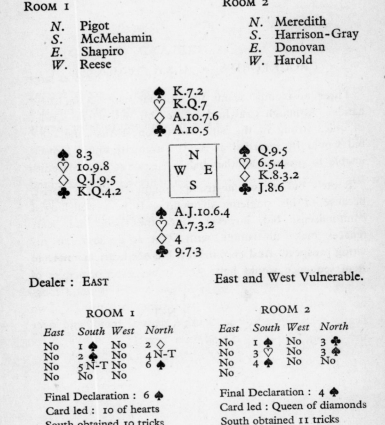

ROOM 1

- *N.* Pigot
- *S.* McMehamin
- *E.* Shapiro
- *W.* Reese

ROOM 2

- *N.* Meredith
- *S.* Harrison-Gray
- *E.* Donovan
- *W.* Harold

♠ K.7.2
♡ K.Q.7
♢ A.10.7.6
♣ A.10.5

♠ 8.3
♡ 10.9.8
♢ Q.J.9.5
♣ K.Q.4.2

♠ Q.9.5
♡ 6.5.4
♢ K.8.3.2
♣ J.8.6

♠ A.J.10.6.4
♡ A.7.3.2
♢ 4
♣ 9.7.3

Dealer : EAST

East and West Vulnerable.

ROOM 1

East	South	West	North
No	1 ♠	No	2 ♢
No	2 ♣	No	4 N-T
No	5 N-T	No	6 ♠
No	No	No	

Final Declaration : 6 ♠
Card led : 10 of hearts
South obtained 10 tricks
E-W + 100

ROOM 2

East	South	West	North
No	1 ♠	No	3 ♣
No	3 ♡	No	3 ♠
No	4 ♠	No	No
No			

Final Declaration : 4 ♠
Card led : Queen of diamonds
South obtained 11 tricks
N-S + 450

NET RESULT OF BOARD + 550 TO GT. BRITAIN

GT. BRITAIN *v.* IRELAND (BOARD 22)

This hand has several lessons. Firstly, on a hand as large as the North hand, Acol always forces. Once a forcing response has been made, North can back-pedal, but if a one-over-one response is made, it is difficult to subsequently show the full strength.

Contrast the bidding of North in the two rooms. Meredith having forced, gives a simple preference on the next round and then passes four spades. The Irish North makes a delicate one-over-one response, but launches into four no-trumps on the next round.

Note also the tendency to rebid the spades in order to show a weak opening bid. Acol is based on principles of common sense. If the rebid of two spades is not strong, no more can any bid *below* two spades be strong. Two hearts therefore becomes South's natural rebid, and over the forcing take-out, he bids three hearts.

GT. BRITAIN *v.* ICELAND (Board 23)

ROOM 1	ROOM 2
N. Meredith	*N.* Johannesson
S. Reese	*S.* Thorfinsson
E. Bergthorsson	*E.* Konstam
W. Karlsson	*W.* Harrison-Gray

♠ A.6.3.2
♡ K.J.10.7
◇ Q.2
♣ 10.9.7

♠ K.8
♡ 9.6
◇ 10.7.4.3
♣ K.Q.J.8.4

	N	
W		E
	S	

♠ Q.9.7.5
♡ Q.4.3
◇ A.6.5
♣ 5.3.2

♠ J.10.4
♡ A.8.5.2
◇ K.J.9.8
♣ A.6

Dealer : SOUTH   Game All.

ROOM 1

South	West	North	East
1 ♡	No	3 ♡	No
No	No		

Final Declaration : 3 ♡
Card led : King of clubs
South obtained 9 tricks
N-S + 140

ROOM 2

South	West	North	East
1 ♡	No	1 ♠	No
2 ◇	No	3 ♡	No
4 ♡	No	No	No

Final Declaration : 4 ♡
Card led : King of clubs
South obtained 8 tricks
E-W + 200

NET RESULT OF BOARD + 340 TO GT. BRITAIN

GT. BRITAIN v. ICELAND (BOARD 23)

An illustration of the Acol " limit " raise. When North raises to three hearts, South, with a minimum opening bid, passes. In the other room North makes a delicate one-over-one response and then bids three hearts. South now has to guess — he is influenced by the fact that his agreement for partner's spade suit may fill the necessary gap. The odds are very heavily against a four-heart contract on the hand.

GT. BRITAIN v. ICELAND (BOARD 29)

ROOM 1

N. Johannsson
S. Thorfinsson
E. Konstam
W. Harrison-Gray

ROOM 2

N. Meredith
S. Reese
E. Bergthorsson
W. Karlsson

```
            ♠ Q.J.10.7.6.4
            ♡ 4
            ◇ 9.6
            ♣ A.Q.10.6
♠ 8.3                        ♠ K
♡ K.Q.10.5.3      N          ♡ A.J.9.6
◇ A.Q.10.3.2   W     E       ◇ J.7.5
♣ J                 S        ♣ 9.7.4.3.2
            ♠ A.9.5.2
            ♡ 8.7.2
            ◇ K.8.4
            ♣ K.8.5
```

Dealer : NORTH   Game All.

ROOM 1

North	East	South	West
No	No	1 ♣	1 ♡
2 ♠	3 ♡	3 ♣	4 ◇
4 ♠	5 ♡	No	No
5 ♣	No	No	No

Final Declaration : 5 ♠
Card led : Ace of hearts
North obtained 10 tricks
E-W + 100

ROOM 2

North	East	South	West
1 ♠	No	2 ♠	3 ♡
4 ♠	No	No	No

Final Declaration : 4 ♠
Card led : Ace of hearts
North obtained 10 tricks
N-S + 620

NET RESULT OF BOARD + 720 TO GT. BRITAIN

GT. BRITAIN *v.* ICELAND (BOARD 29)

A triumph for the light Acol opening bid. Note that in Room 1 North passes with his six-loser hand (presumably because he is deficient in honour tricks) while South, with his nine-loser hand opens the bidding. Konstam, however, grasped his opportunity of showing his heart support at the three level and the Icelandic pair had eventually to make a sacrifice against five hearts which would have made.

In the other room North (Meredith) opens one spade — a typical Acol opening bid. When his partner can only say two spades, he realises that the opponents must have a good heart contract and makes the splendid semi-defensive bid of four spades.

GT. BRITAIN v. BELGIUM (BOARD 24)

ROOM 1   ROOM 2

    N. Finkelstein   *N.* Meredith
    S. de Henricourt   *S.* Reese
    E. Konstam   *E.* Savostine
    W. Harrison-Gray   *W.* Furgern

```
                    ♠ K.8
                    ♡ A.Q.8.2
                    ◇ A.K.J.6.4.3
                    ♣ 10

  ♠ J.6              ┌─────────┐      ♠ Q.5.4
  ♡ K.6.5.4          │    N    │      ♡ J.9.7.3
  ◇ 10.9          W  │         │  E   ◇ Q.7.2
  ♣ Q.9.8.4.3        │    S    │      ♣ A.J.2
                     └─────────┘

                    ♠ A.10.9.7.3.2
                    ♡ 10
                    ◇ 8.5
                    ♣ K.7.6.5
```

Dealer : WEST   Love All.

ROOM 1					ROOM 2			
West	*North*	*East*	*South*		*West*	*North*	*East*	*South*
No	1 ◇	No	1 ♠		No	1 ◇	No	1 ♠
No	2 ♡	No	2 ♠		No	2 ♡	No	2 ♠
No	3 ◇	No	No		No	3 ♠	No	4 ♠
No					No	No	No	

Final Declaration : 3 ◇   Final Declaration : 4 ♠
Card led : Ace of clubs   Card led : 4 of clubs
North obtained 11 tricks   South obtained 10 tricks
N-S + 150   N-S + 420

NET RESULT OF BOARD + 270 TO GT. BRITAIN

GT. BRITAIN v. BELGIUM (BOARD 24)

A good many modern systems tend to use a reverse bid artificially and as completely forcing. The Acol principle is much more natural — the diamond bid before the hearts *guarantees* that the diamond suit is longer and so that fact does not need reaffirming. The reverse bid is strong but it is not an *absolute* force. The two spade bid by Reese therefore shows some values and Meredith is able to make the key bid of three spades.